Pom

Part one - Growing Pains

1954-1960

George East

Pompey Lad

Part one - Growing Pains 1954-1960

Published by La Puce Publications

© George East 2022

website: www.george-east.net

Typesetting and design by Francesca Brooks

paperback edition ISBN 978-1-908747-80-8
kindle edition ISBN: 978-1-908747-81-5
e-Pub edition ISBN: 978-1-908747-79-2

Author's Note

This is the second book in what was planned to be a series of one (*Just a Pompey Boy*). This one is the first of two books covering my transition from a mostly innocent primary school boy to a fully fledged tearaway, living on drugs, rock 'n' roll and as much sex as I could lay my hands on. I should add that in those days and even for a fervent what we used to call 'knobhound' like myself, it was not easy to get more than half a leg-over.

As the title suggests, the series is about me, but more so about life in Portsmouth - or anywhere else in the country at a very special time. My youthful escapades were perhaps a bit extreme, but I think my experiences and adventures were broadly similar to millions of young men and women. It was, of course, a time when British society changed so dramatically from the grey post-war years to what seemed to many a new and exciting world.

Whether you believe it was a change for the better or worse will I think depend on your age, attitude and how much fun you had in those far-off days.

The Music of Life

As with most of my generation, popular music was a constant and irreplaceable companion on my journey into adulthood.

Apart from novelty children's songs and tunes like *The Runaway Train Came Over the Hill* and *I Taut I Saw a Puddy Tat*, music played no great part in my early years. Then my adolescent juices were stirred by the arrival of the great god Rock 'n' Roll in the shape of the hour-glass-figured Jayne Mansfield sashaying down the road to Little Richard's thumping accompaniment in that most classic of pop movies, *The Girl Can't Help it*. Being only 12, I wasn't sure why, but I found the music - and Ms Mansfield - very exciting.

From then on there were pop songs and tunes to suit my every mood or situation. Songs and tunes for times when I lost the girl I had loved for a week or two, or for when I had just met the new love of my life. There were also great songs and tunes to cheer me up when I was down, and to put me in the mood for dancing, drinking, fighting and, especially, having sex.

The hits I have listed at the start of each year are just a sample of the sort of music and artists we liked then. I've also included snatches of the lyrics from songs that moved me most at the time and have stayed with me across the years. There were hundreds of hits to choose from, and if you are roughly of the same vintage as me, I hope some of them meant as much to you as they did to me.

Bite-size Pompey

For those who've not had the pleasure of acquaintance with our fair city and to set the scene for the forthcoming action, here's a snapshot of Pompey's past and present:

- Emerging from coastal marshlands at the end of the 11th century, Portsmouth became the nation's premier naval port because of location and the foresight of monarchs and military leaders going back as far as the Roman Occupation. Often confused with Plymouth and other naval ports, Portsmouth is probably best known as the place from whence Admiral Nelson sallied forth in 1805 to beat up the French at the Battle of Trafalgar. Soccer fans may know Pompey as the only team ever to have held the FA Cup for seven years (World War II got in the way), and from some legendary players… and for the notorious 6.57 Crew 'supporters' club.

- Famous sons or sometime residents of the city include engineer Isambard Kingdom Brunel, former Prime Minister James Callaghan, movie star and intellectual Arnold Schwarzenegger and a whole library's-worth of writers from Charles Dickens to Rudyard Kipling, H. G. Wells, Sir Arthur Conan Doyle. And, of course, me.

- 'Pompey' hangs like a glittering jewel or, some might say, snotty dewdrop from the coastline of Hampshire, and is the only island city in the

United Kingdom. A lot of people must like or at least have a reason for living there, as the population density is pretty much the highest in the UK. Portsea Island (which most people think of as Portsmouth) has an area of under twenty-five square miles and a population of more than 200,000. To make a basic comparison, coming up for 150 people occupy every square kilometre in Wales. In Pompey it is a tad over 5000. Yep, that's *five thousand*.

- Despite this enforced cheek-to-jowl neighbourliness, Pomponians can be very welcoming to outsiders, unless they diss our fair city or hail from Southampton.

- Like all naval ports, Pompey has long played host to peoples and ships from around the world. We were multi-cultural before it was trendy, and that must have contributed significantly to the city's character and culture. Then there's how our seagoing history has resulted in Portsmouth having its own accent, and even language. For centuries, young men from inland locations across Britain would be drawn by exotic tales of roving the seven seas to come to Portsmouth and join the Royal Navy. They would then marry a local girl and start a family. Across the centuries, this has enriched the city's range of traditions, attitudes and even vocabulary as you can see at the end of the book.

- Together with its unique island status, Pompey has some interesting firsts and lasts, like for example:

- The first-ever UFO sighting in Britain to be recognised and investigated by the Ministry of Defence occurred over Portsmouth in 1950

- Sir Arthur Conan Doyle attended his first séance in Portsmouth and was converted to Spiritualism in 1887, the year the first Sherlock Holmes novel was published

- Arrested in Portsmouth in 1944, Helen Duncan was the last woman in Britain to be charged with Conjuring Spirits under the 1735 Witchcraft Act

- The first dry dock in England was built in Portsmouth in 1497

- Tobacco was first smoked in England on Portsmouth High Street in 1604. Legend has it that a woman thought the sailors having a smoke were on fire and threw the contents of a chamber pot over them.

Prologue:

The story of this part of my and the city's life begins in 1954. The war had ended less than a decade before, and Portsmouth was recovering from the damage like a boxer after a successful but damaging bout. We'd won the fight, but the bruises were still on show.

Speed, pragmatism and cost were the driving forces, and 'regeneration' was well under way. Basically, that meant repairing much of the damage and providing new homes for those survivors dispossessed of a roof over their heads by the Portsmouth Blitz. Cubist blocks of flats and pre-fabricated homes were sprouting from bomb sites where rows of terraced homes, shops and some striking Victorian pubs, theatres, churches and governmental buildings once stood. Bland in comparison they might be, but the new homes had indoor toilets and even bathrooms, and the city was building for the future. Sadly, none of the architectural splendours of past times could be replaced.

Although on the move, Portsmouth in the 1950s was still a grey, grimy place, and life had not changed much for ordinary people for a generation or two. A house with a car parked outside was still a rarity, and Dad still went to work on his bike. TVs, fridges and washing machines were far from the norm and Mum would be in charge of all things to do with shopping, cleaning, feeding the family and disciplining the children. In her spare time, the little woman would be expected to take on home maintenance up to and including renewing roof tiles or re-plastering a crumbling wall.

But, things were going to change as we headed for a new decade, and the change would be much more dramatic than most people could possibly have imagined.

I couldn't wait for this brave new day to dawn, as I was just back from what I hoped had been a peek into the future.

~

It was my second year at the Technical High School, and, apart from summer camps on the Isle of Wight, I'd been on my first trip abroad. The school exchange trip to Paris made me realise how different life was across the Channel for young people, and how much I would like to be like them.

Although 'teenagers' had been officially recognised in America since 1944, young people in Britain were still expected to be seen and mostly not heard, to know their place and dress, look and act like their Mums and Dads had. Whichever way you looked at it, Post-War Britain was a pretty drab place. TV programmes were black and white. and that seemed the colour of life.

But there was hope for a more colourful future. Apart from pimples, a sprinkling of hairs around the willy and wet dreams, adolescence brought with it the overwhelming urge to be as unlike our parents as possible. We didn't know what we were rebelling against and to what end, but we wanted to be different. It hadn't happened before, or was simply not acknowledged by society. Sociologists have dubbed our parents as the Silent Generation, and our children Generation X. For good or ill, we baby boomers were to set the pattern for every subsequent generation so have only ourselves to blame.

I had spent weeks before the French trip working on my cool Elvis sneer and practising the French for 'What you looking at, mush?' We had to wear our school macs, but turned the collars up and pretended to have forgotten to bring the belts so as to look cool. We also had to wear blazers and regulation grey flannel trousers, but made up for it with rebelliously lurid and even fluorescent Teddy-boy style socks. And joy of joys, we were allowed to leave our caps at home. Brylcreem jars were emptied in the process of creating Bill Hayley kiss curls and Elvis quiffs, and Chopper Wilson sold some of the boys what he said were called French Letters. It was not likely we would get to use them for their true purpose, he said, but it was cool to 'accidentally' let the small brown envelope drop from your wallet when with your mates. He closed the deal by saying they were also great for blowing up and slipping in amongst the balloons at little kids' birthday parties.

~

Apart from them eating frogs, smoking really smelly fags and stinking of garlic, none of our party knew much about our Gallic neighbours, and that seemed to include the teacher who took our French lessons. Our phrase books were limited to Madelaine and Suzette asking Jean-Michel if he fancied a row on the river, and our knowledge of French culture was picked up from what we heard in the playground about how General de Gaulle's willy was as oversized as his nose.

During the Napoleonic Wars a mob hanged a monkey at Folkestone in the belief it was a French spy, and we were not much better informed. Apart from eating and smoking habits, we knew the French never washed, always peed in public and were not as good as us at fighting, but that was about it. We also knew we'd liberated their country in the War, but they seemed to resent our help rather than be properly grateful.

From the moment the coach left the ferry port at Dieppe, we could see we were in another country, and one where things were done very differently. This was even more so when we arrived in Paris. Everything and everyone seemed to move faster than at home, the policemen wore funny hats and moustaches and short capes and swung their batons to tell people and traffic where to go. Not that anyone seemed to pay any attention. I had known they drove on the wrong side of the road in France, but in Paris they seemed to drive anywhere they liked, especially around the Arc de Triomphe. The cars were amazing, with sleek Citroëns crouching like tigers by the kerb or racing recklessly along the boulevard. Then there were the weird 'two horses' Deux Chevaux cars and delivery vans, which looked like they had been knocked up from the corrugated iron sheets of old Anderson shelters.

The most noticeable aspect of the French capital for me was that the air was thick with the smell of acrid cigarettes, garlic, stale urine and unwashed bodies.

Cool and the gang. Me and the boys outside a Paris bar, trying very hard to look the business. Note the shades and the fag hanging nonchalantly from my lips, despite the fact I had not yet started smoking.

Given the hygiene standards of the time, the B.O. was not that shocking, but garlic and *Gauloises* fags were pretty much unknown where I came from, and mostly it was only matelots on a runashore in Pompey who pissed in the streets.

~

Billeted in a posh boarding school in the centre of Paris, we quickly learned that, despite what they liked to think, the French were clearly not much good at cooking or organising meals.

At breakfast the bread came in long sticks rather than proper sandwich shapes, and the coffee in metal bowls with no handles. Even stranger, the main meal was not served the proper way with everything together on one plate, but as separate courses. The meat would arrive, and was always undercooked and even leaking blood. Then the potatoes, with a handful of skinny beans which had been boiled to within an inch of their lives. When I asked one of the cooks if there were any other vegetables, he looked outraged and said that, unlike the British, his countrymen did not care to have an allotment on their plates.

But to me and my mates, the overwhelming difference and most exciting aspect of the trip was how Parisians of our age dressed, looked and acted. They really were from a different planet, and we longed to be like them.

The boys wore short, stylish 'Perry Como' haircuts and round-necked Pringle-style sweaters in bright colours, sta-prest trousers and really, really smart moccasin-like slip-on shoes. They even smoked unconcernedly and very stylishly in front of adults, and, most envy-making of all, zipped about on buzzy mopeds with their girlfriends languidly draped side-saddle behind them. One of the boys said he had heard they even drank wine with their parents at meals,

On our last evening I sat on the bed in my dormitory cubicle and gazed for the hundredth time at the poster on the partition wall. Obviously left there by the regular occupant, it showed actress Brigitte Bardot pouting at the camera. She was obviously naked, her golden hair tumbling down across her shapely shoulders and barely covering her breasts. We had Vivien Leigh and Audrey Hepburn and even Joan Collins, but they just didn't seem to match the allure of The Sex Kitten.

On the coach home, I sat in a near-stupor and thought about what it must be like to live in such a place as Paris, or anywhere in France. I knew for certain that I wanted to live there one day and get my fill of freedom and liberty. And mostly of sex, perhaps even with Brigitte Bardot. Except for the sex with the Sex Kitten, my wishes would come true in later life. But for now, it was back to black-and-white Britain.

1954

Those were the Days

~ Roger Bannister becomes the first man to break the four-minute mile. Diane Leather becomes the first woman to break the five-minute mile
~ Fourteen years of rationing during and after WWII ends when meat is officially taken off ration
~ The IRA signals the renewal of activity with an arms raid on a barracks in Armagh
~ The Wolfenden Committee is set up to report on homosexuality and prostitution in Britain
~ BBC Television broadcasts the first episode of Fabian of the Yard
~ The first Wimpy Bar in the UK is opened in London
~ Future singing stars Elvis Costello, Annie Lennox and Joe Jackson are born
~ JRR Tolkien publishes the first two books in the Lord of the Rings trilogy
~ Successful films of the year include The Sea Shall Not Have Them, The Dam Busters, Animal Farm and The Belles of St Trinians, starring Alistair Sim
~ Johnny Dankworth and his 20-piece Orchestra appeared at the Savoy Ballroom, Southsea
~ Larry Adler and the Southern Philharmonic Orchestra appeared at the King's Theatre, Southsea

Top Tunes

I saw Mummy kissing Santa Claus ~ The Beverley Sisters

Answer Me ~ David Whitfield and (separately*) Frankie Laine

Oh Mein Papa ~ Eddie Calvert and (separately) Eddie Fisher

Swedish Rhapsody ~ Mantovani and (separately) Ray Martin

Three Coins in the Fountain ~ The Four Aces and (separately) Frank Sinatra

Friends and Neighbours ~ Billy Cotton and his Band

If I Give My Heart to You ~ Doris Day

Sh-Boom ~ The Crew Cats

That's Amoré ~ Dean Martin

Chicka Boom ~ Guy Mitchell

This Old House ~ Rosemary Clooney

Heartbeat ~ Ruby Murray

The Happy Wanderer ~ The Obernkirchen Children's Choir

Don't Laugh at Me ('cause I'm a Fool') - Norman Wisdom

Although it seems peculiar nowadays, it was quite common in the 1950s for the same song to be in the charts by two or even more separate artists. Often but not always, one would be a cover version of an American hit by a British performer. Purists or Americanophiles invariably went for the Trans-Atlantic original.

I love to go a-wandering,
Along the mountain track,
And as I go, I love to sing,
My knapsack on my back.
Val-deri, Val-dera,
Val-deri,
Val-dera-ha-ha-ha-ha-ha
Val-deri,Val-dera.
My knapsack on my back.

The Happy Wanderer by The Obernkirchen
Children's Choir
Lyrics by Friedrich-Wilhelm Möller

Frensham Road was (and still is) a pleasant, tree-lined thoroughfare close to Fratton Park, home of Portsmouth Football Club. Number 31 was to be the new family home and business, and I had mixed feelings about the move.

For me, the change from a decidedly quirky boarding house in Southsea to a corner shop in Milton had its up and downsides. I'd lost my gang and my seaside playground, but it would be a new adventure and I'd at last have a room all to myself. The house in Castle Road was a big place, but Mother hated turning B & B business away and accommodations had to be made. When the need called, brother John and I had to share a room, or, in extreme cases, the garden shed.

On the debit side we were moving downhill in location, but not much. Like most cities, Portsmouth is a collection of former villages, and each had its status ranking. Southsea came at the top of the snob-appeal hit parade, Landport, Buckland and Fratton at the bottom. Curiously, although Eastney sat cheek-to jowl with Southsea beside the sea, it was not a place to boast about living in. Milton was somewhere in the middle, depending on what part of the former village you lived in.

Nowadays and thanks to the inventiveness of estate agents and the value that a sexy address can put on the most ordinary of houses, Eastney has become East Southsea or even Eastney Village, while I note that Frensham Road has somehow upped sticks and crossed the border from Milton into Southsea.

~

I remember that day as a whirl of activity as Mother harried the removal men and dad rolled a fag, dreamed his dreams of owning the next Mick the Miller*, studied form in *The Sporting Life* and sensibly kept out of the way.

The first job was to squeeze the furniture we had brought with us into the back room, which led on to a small kitchen and lean-to. There was no stock room apart from the cupboard under the stairs, but that was no immediate problem as we had no stock. Upstairs were three bedrooms and - wonder of the age - a bathroom and inside toilet. I was not sure whether I was happy or sad at the prospect of no more communal zinc bath nights in front of the kitchen fire.

Mother and dad would have the front bedroom,

and John and I slugged it out for first choice of the other two. He said he should have automatic right of choice as he was the oldest. I said the smaller one would suit him as he spent hardly any time in the house, let alone his room. He was only fourteen but was already 'into' girls and out gallivanting at youth clubs and milk bars every night. In the end I won after threatening to tell mum about the Health & Efficiency magazine I knew he kept under the rag-rug beside his bed.

~

The next month sped by as my parents prepared to open the doors of Kay's Store.

Sensibly, the division of labour was for Mother to look after the planning, stock selection, ordering, and marketing, while dad was responsible (under her direction) for the DIY, painting, bodging and heavy lifting work.

Meanwhile, I was serving my final term at Cottage Grove. This meant commuting by bus and spending time after school on my beloved bombsite adventure playgrounds, which were a facility noticeably absent in Milton.

One evening I arrived home to find a strange man eating a tin of cat food and pretending to like it. He wasn't barking mad, but a salesman who wanted to show how wholesome his product was. I felt sorry for him when Mother let him finish the tin before saying she had already done a deal with the man from Whiskas.

Shelves were being put up and everything painted, including my father. He wasn't much of a hand with a saw or a brush, but as Mother said, he was cheap and easily bullied. It was all pretty basic, as finances did not stretch to a freezer, which was a drawback. Frozen food was not on the menu of most corner shops then, but it meant the shop would only be able to offer ice lollies in the depths of winter. It was to be my job to fill the moulds with syrup and stack them on the window ledge in the yard. Amazingly, they sold best on the coldest days.

Outside, the newly-painted shop front was a gleaming combination of royal blue, orchard green, muddy brown and a very red, red. This was not a design feature aiming to attract maximum attention, but the using-up of a lot of half-empty tins from the shed at Castle Road.

Above the main window, the name of Mother's new venture had been boldly proclaimed in the bright blue, augmented with banana yellow. Again, money had been saved by letting dad do the signage. As he had never written any signs and was no great hand at writing letters, the project was more or less doomed from the outset. Unsurprisingly, dad didn't bother with much pre-planning or laying-out of the lettering, but got stuck straight in with a two-inch brush. This meant the letters got smaller and closer together towards the end, and the 'y' in Kay's Stores lost its tail completely. Several passers-by stopped to ask who Kav was, probably suspicious of a foreign owner. Ever resourceful, Mother used any enquiries as an opportunity to steer the potential customers into the shop to look around. They were not allowed off the premises until they had given her their addresses and promises to be regular patrons. I don't know what the original plan was, but the final choice of what the shop would sell seemed based on a mixture of circumstance, availability and budget.

Fratton Park was less than a mile away and with thousands of people passing by or near the shop on match days, the basic offerings were, as they say nowadays, a no-brainer. There was no licence for newspaper vending, but Kay's was allowed to sell cigarettes. Confectionery, soft drinks and snacks were also a must, and on match days Mother even laid out a window display of rosettes and badges and other Portsmouth FC favours. She knew that an army of fans would pass the window before arriving outside the ground where the favours were officially on sale. She was also canny enough to post me or dad as look-outs in case rival fans made their noisy way towards the shop. In that case, the Pompey favours would be swiftly removed from the window before the visitors arrived and ordered their packets of Woodbines or Weights fags and steak pies or pork and dripping rolls.

To local residents, Kay's would also be selling tinned goods and groceries and anything else which could be crammed into the available space. The only comestibles not on offer were fruit and vegetables. This was ostensibly so as not to tread on the toes of the greengrocer next door, but mostly because Mother had seen how little profit there was in a pound of spuds and a rapidly wilting lettuce.

Apart from Mr. Weekes, our bear-like but amiable neighbour, the only other shop was at the other end of Frensham Road. Barely visible through the grubby window was a half-hearted display of some tired-looking balls of wool and faded pre-war knitting patterns and it was said locally that the last customer seen entering the premises was before the War. Nowadays, former or failed shops are instantly turned into houses; in those days people just lived in them as they were and hoped someone might come in and buy whatever they put in the window.

Kay's Store was busy from the opening day, because, as usual, Mother had done her homework, seen what the area was missing, and provided it.

After stocking the shop to the limit of her budget and filling any shelf space with empty sweet tins and fake packets of cigarettes, she was ready for the grand opening. I remember my dad cautiously testing the till, which was definitely of pre-war vintage, and probably the Boer War. It looked like something you would see on the counter of a Dickensian haberdashery store, was made of wood and shaped like a miniature coffin. At one end was a brass handle to pull the cash drawer out, and on the top was a glass panel with a slot in it, giving access to a roll of paper. The idea was to write down the amount of each transaction, then open the drawer. A little bell would ring and the paper reel would move on a fraction. It was noticeable how rarely either my mother or father actually noted down a sale or the amount taken for it. As Mother said when I asked her about it, she and dad were the only two using the till, and, besides, she had a very good memory, so it would be a waste of paper and pencil lead to note the transactions down. As I eventually figured out, it would also avoid any unpleasant en-counters with the Tax Man. Back then, the only books kept by most small shops were from the library.

~

As the proprietor of what she described as a general store, Mother refused to wear an apron or overall, and always opened the shop looking as if she was off on a swish night out. She rightly figured it would gain respect from the female customers, and admiration from the men.

When on duty in the evenings, Dad would wear a white coat of the sort barbers and scientists affected, and had written the name of the shop on the top pocket in red ink. It had soaked into the material and wasn't very legible, but at least there was room to complete the loop on the 'y'.

In those days, advertising was very much a low-key affair for local businesses, and the announcement of the opening was limited to a hand-made poster in the window. My mother, being who she was, also knocked on every door in Frensham Road and beyond, introducing herself and telling the potential customers what would be on special offer for the first week of opening.

I didn't know or much care how well the business was doing, but the bell on the top of the door seemed to jangle regularly and once they were in, it wasn't easy to leave without a purchase, even if they had rushed in to ask to use the phone because of an emergency at home. Like Arkwright in Open All Hours or Auntie Wainwright in the junk shop in Last of the Summer Wine, Mother was very good at not letting customers leave without taking more than they had come in for.

~

Although the shop seemed to be going well, it wasn't long before Mother suggested my dad looked for a day job. There was no call or room for two people behind the counter, and he usually took the evening shift. With his height, dark good looks and ready wit, he was popular with the customers, and I think Mother sometimes thought he was a bit too popular with the female customers of a certain age. Looking back, I suspect she was torn between the irritation of seeing dad's lady fans fawn over him, and pleasure at the value of the extra income he could coax out of an admirer.

Whatever the motivation, dad found or was found a job as a bread and cakes roundsman for a local bakery. This was another shrewd move by Mother, as Kay's Stores was a customer of Dyke's bakery, and dad delivered her order at the end of his round. I don't think Mother would have allowed actual larceny, but I know there were always lots of past-their-best fancy cakes and buns and loaves on show in the shop. They were sold at reduced prices, and I suspect the price to Mother was extremely favourable.

My time at Cottage Grove was coming to an end, the 11-plus Examination loomed. Whatever the result, I would soon be making another move from familiar, comfortable surroundings.

At our last meeting before the end of term, the Castle Road Knights voted unanimously that I should continue to be a full member no matter where I went to school or lived for the rest of my life. In an emotional moment we swore that nothing would break our bond, though once again we chickened out from sealing the oath with our blood.

It was a solemn moment and, young as we were, I think that we all realised that leaving Cottage Grove meant we were moving towards childhood's end.

~

Life went on as normal in those final weeks, but I was bemused how the girls in our class seemed the most upset at our imminent parting. Some of them would come to see me on the bus or bike after school, and Samantha Stott, the front bottom flasher (*see Just a Pompey Boy part I*) would actually pedal the three miles several times a week to bring me a bag of sweets.

When I asked my mother why she thought that a girl would come all that way to give a bag of sherbet lemons to a boy who lived in a sweet shop, she smiled, then said, as I'd find out when I grew up, girls were not, in some respects, at all like boys.

Mick the Miller is probably the most famous racing greyhound of all time. He was born in 1926 in Ireland, owned by a Catholic priest, and remains a legend to millions of dog racing fans.

Play Up Pompey

On home game days you could hear the roar from Fratton Park as if it were just across the road, which in fact it was.

Tens of thousands of supporters would descend on Portsmouth FC's home ground hours before kick-off, many to get a few pints of watery beer down them before the off. To appreciate the excitement and what a big event it was, you need to remember how little leisure time and entertainment was available to the average working man then. Pompey was his team and a home match was almost as eagerly anticipated as Christmas for a child. In those good old days of Pompey riding high in the First Division, a crowd of up to fifty thousand would turn up to cheer on their side and boo the unpopular players on the other team. There was always a pantomime ankle-breaking or shoulder-crunching villain, and seeing him doing his stuff or getting his comeuppance was part of the fun. A win would send the locals home happy; a defeat could cast a pall over the coming week.

In my memory's eye, I see the scene on a match day as a sort of Lowry-esqe painting, except that amongst the horde of figures in identical drab clothes and cloth caps would be the black hats and tally bands of sailors. As none but a handful of ratings would be natives of Portsmouth and most from north of the Watford Gap, the cheering for a goal by the away team would sometimes equal that of a Pompey strike. Noticeably, the drawn-out 'Ooooohs' in reaction to a near-miss from either side would be almost as loud as the cheers for a goal.

Setting up shop so close to Fratton Park was all part of Mother's grand plan, and on match days, sweets, snacks and cigarette sales would rocket. Chocolate bars, cakes and filled rolls would fly off the shelves, sometimes literally if Mother and dad were under pressure behind the counter. Cheese rolls were on sale at Fratton Park, but the fans knew that the snack bar was quite near to the truly odiferous toilet block. As a former boarding house proprietor, Mother also knew the way to excite a soccer fan's taste buds.

The day before the game, she would roast a joint of belly pork and order a couple of trays of crusty bread rolls. Next morning, the rolls would be 'buttered' with the dripping and filled with a thick slice of fatty pork. Lots of pepper and salt would be added, and favoured customers would get a piece of crackling as a bonus.

Although I was never a football fan, I'd feel the air

of anticipation and excitement in the streets as kick-off time approached. Soccer had arrived in the town in the mid-19th century with dockers and sailors from the North, and Portsmouth FC was founded in 1898. After an unremarkable history, Pompey had won the FA cup in 1939 and the Division One title for two consecutive years from 1948-50. Now the team was riding high and enjoying what would be later known as their 'glory days'. The record attendance was a massive 51,385, and an average crowd would exceed 35,000. Nowadays it struggles to beat 15,000.

Although I shared Mother's disinterest, Dad and John were keen followers of the Blues, and would hurry to the ground after the rush was over. Sometimes they would take me along, and I found the spectacle rather than the game of the most interest.

For a ten-year-old hanging on to his father and brother's hands, it was quite an experience to be swept along in the midst of an ever-swelling crowd at fart level, the air thick with cigarette smoke, beery and other fumes, chants and shouts and the crackle of rattles and hoots from horns. In those pre-deodorant days, the smell of the crowd would probably have rivalled the roar, but we were all the same so few would have noticed.

Programme, rosette and souvenir sellers marked the route, each displaying their wares on a board fixed to a long pole like a Roman Legionnaire holding the Eagle proudly aloft.

There would be a police presence lining the route from Fratton Station and other approach points, but physical violence was rare. This was in spite of the away fans being allowed to mingle with home supporters. To my memory and bearing in mind how the game was played in those days, it would be true to say there was usually more violence on the field than off it, especially if Jimmy Scoular was playing.

Having paid and squeezed through the turnstile, dad and John would ignore the stewards with their lollipop sticks marking where there was room, and shove into their favoured station on the half-way line. As there was no seating for the rank-and-file supporters, they would lean against a metal barrier similar to an oversized bike rack. I would be shepherded with other small children down to the cinder track surrounding the pitch. There we could sit and watch the action, play five-stones, swap cigarette cards or throw handfuls of coke at each other.

Whenever I think back to those far-away, long-gone Saturday afternoons, I see the scene in black and white. On a cold or wet day, standard dress for civilians would be lengthy, grey, belted gabardine mackintoshes, often threadbare woollen overcoats or donkey jackets over grey flannels and black shoes or boots. Those civilians with heads covered would be wearing a rumpled cloth cap or, occasionally, a homburg or trilby hat. In today's rainbow and individualistic world, it is difficult to understand how comfortably conformist we were then. Men were at home in their tweedy hacking jackets or old and patched suit coats, while sons wore school blazers or jackets like their dad's. A note to all feminists and modern-day female fans: I haven't mentioned women in the crowd, because I don't remember seeing any.

As the latecomers squeezed in and the gates closed, the pre-match entertainment would begin.

The star performer was a man with a tray of sharp-tasting, allegedly medicinal pastilles, who made his appearance to almost as big a welcome as would greet the teams. He was known as Old Herbal and had a catchphrase which had become a crowd chant in its own right. His first piercing 'Cough No More!' would be cheered to the grandstand rafters.

Apart from his catchphrase, Old Herbal's particular skill was to throw a packet of pastilles from the cinder track to any part of the ground with unerring accuracy. The money, like the small children, would be safely handed down the terrace, the customer would stick his hand up and the bag would sail through the air. Catching it cleanly would earn a bonus cheer in the way of a crowd catch at a cricket ground.

Then the buzz would die down while the pre-match announcements were made on the tinny-sounding loudspeakers. It would be mostly team information and I particularly recall the ironic cheer when Blackpool were our guests and the news would come that Stanley Matthews would not be taking to the field. Whether or not it was true, it was said that the great Stanley (later Sir Stanley) Matthews was, in local parlance 'trash' to play because he knew he would be targeted by a couple of the team's fearsome hard men. One was left back Harry Ferrier and the other was one of the most combative players in the league. Jimmy Scoular's nickname was The Volcano, because of his incendiary eruptions if things didn't go his way. He was said to attack the man with the ball like a runaway coal wagon, and this was in the days when anything short of a broken limb was regarded as fair play.

At last, the teams would enter the field of battle to a huge roar and cacophony of noise from rattles and hooters. Though they were local heroes, most of the home players would be on not much more than the average wage, and when their playing days were over would usually take a Portsmouth pub to make a living. But for these shining moments with the adoring roar of thousands of fans ringing in their ears, they were kings.

At half time, the marching bands of either the Royal Marines or the Portsmouth Fire Brigade would take to the field. The Marines were brilliant and the Fire Brigade rubbish, and both would have to compete with a deafening rendition of the Pompey Chimes from the terraces. At the same time there would be a rush to the very basic urinals and the snack bar alongside. The cheese in the rolls was said to have been stolen from the mousetraps in the local orphanage, and the running joke about the meat pies was that visiting supporters would think that the green bits in them was cabbage.

Meanwhile, a host of beer-swollen-bladdered men would be queuing for a place at the urinal trough in the nearby toilet. To this day I can't lift a mug of beef extract to my lips without recalling the pungent combination of the sharp tang of Bovril mixed with the rank odour of hundreds of beery men relieving themselves in a place as dark and noisome as the Black Hole of Calcutta.

Though only a couple of miles away from our old home in Castle Road, Milton was almost foreign territory. Another aspect of life in the city then would seem risible to young Pomponians. It was that people were much more parochial then, and in both senses of the word. Before we all became 'liberated' and well-travelled because of the motor car and cheap foreign travel, most people worked and shopped and pubbed and danced and courted where they lived. They really did often marry the boy or girl next door, or at least no more than a few streets away. For some oldies, a trip beyond the invisible boundary lines of their parish was a small adventure, and I knew some who never left home turf from birth to death.

Because of where it was, bomb damage was relatively rare in this part of the city, and apart from when Pompey were playing home, Milton was a quiet and even sedate place to someone more used to the bustle of Southsea.

Although times were on the change, the daily routine and rhythm of life was more or less the same as before the War, and seemed immutable. Dawn would arrive with the milkman and his curiously humming electric float, followed by the baker's roundsman. After a hasty breakfast, dads would clamber on to cycle or motor bike and set off to work, while the lady of the house would see the kids off to school and start her long and busy day at home. 'Housewife' is often seen as a derogatory term nowadays, but it was an accurate one when women were almost as married to their homes as to their husband.

But even tied to her home, the lady of the house

was unlikely to get lonely. There was the lady next door to chat to over the garden wall or have a feud with. Door-to-door salesmen would call regularly with offers of magic cleaning aides or a shelf -load of encyclopaedias. Then there would be the tallyman to collect the rent or the weekly payments for the sofa which had been bought on 'tick', 'the knock' or the 'never-never' (you might have it but it'll never be paid for). These regular cash collectors always arrived by bike, but occupied different levels on the ladder of social status. Those from money-lending or dubious companies always looked furtive, while those from posh furniture shops might wear a bow tie and blazer, and would take their cycle clips off before Madame opened the front door. I remember one who looked a bit like film star Charles Boyer, smoked a pipe and always wore a carnation in his buttonhole. It was said that he could charm the weekly payments (if not more) from the most reluctant housewife.

Other regular callers might include the window cleaner, knife-grinder, rag and bone man or someone to empty the coin-in-the-slot rental TV. In between visits and other household chores, housewives took off their pinnies, put on their hats and coats, took their shopping bags (they were all 'bags-for-life' in those days) from the hook and set out on foot or bike for the daily shop. But there would be regular passing traders, and one of the most popular in Milton was Neller's fruit and veg cart. The family store was in Winter Road, but every day the ruddy-faced Jim would walk his patch alongside the horse, cap on the back of his head and a ready smile as he weighed out and served up the spuds and onions. So, in fact, home deliveries from the likes of Ocado are far from a modern concept.

Another memorable figure on the Milton street scene was the Muffin Man. I remember him as a middle aged, tubby chap, hair plastered back with Brylcreem and wearing a brown, button up overall coat. He worked at the nearby Scott's Bakery, and his job was to tour the streets on a strange contraption consisting of a large box on wheels joined with the back half of a sit-up-and-beg bicycle. The Muffin Man would ring his handbell with a resigned expression as he pedalled laboriously by. I am sure he was a perfectly nice man, but we found him slightly creepy. This was probably because of the rumour spread by older children that, as well as muffins, fancy cakes and fresh bread rolls, the box always had room for a couple of kids to fuel the bakery ovens.

~

As the year and my last term at cottage Grove came to a close, I was beginning to feel almost at home in my new surroundings and had made new friends. Two in particular were to share many of the rites of passage through childhood to adolescence. They would also be instrumental in my first attempt at finding fame and fortune through a rock group.

Mike Beacon was a year younger than me, lived round the corner and was a choirboy at the local church. He was an open-faced easy-going type, and easily bully-able, which suited me. Bobby Harrigan was someone I looked up to in both senses. He was in the second year at the Portsmouth Technical High, tall and slim and so laid-back he looked as if he might fall over in a strong breeze. He had a lazy smile and nothing seemed to faze him. Everyone liked Bobby, and he had promised my mother that he would keep an eye on me at school.

Like most children then, the streets and beaches and open spaces were our playgrounds, and the only time we spent indoors was after dark. Milton Park was nearby, and most afternoons we'd put a couple of sweaters on the grass and play soccer till dusk, when the bell would ring and the parkie come to chuck us out. Some evenings and if we felt daring, we'd wait till he'd locked up and cycled off, then buy threepence worth of chips and scraps and climb over the gate. There we'd feast, sitting in the dark on a bench by the bowling green and vying to come up with the scariest ghost stories. More innocent times, perhaps, but it never occurred to us to cause any damage to make our mark.

Another small adventure was to cycle to the foreshore at Langstone harbour, where the eastern tip of Portsea Island almost met with the western corner of my birthplace, Hayling Island. Nowadays it is a place of soaring apartment blocks overlooking posh marinas and yacht clubs. Then it was a glorious stretch of undeveloped land with a houseboat village and dangerous rip-tides just off shore to risk our lives on with rubber tyres as our motor torpedo boat in pursuit of German subs. The Glory Hole was an area favoured as an unofficial tip, with mountains of brick and concrete rubble and unwanted household furniture and other detritus. It was as close as this part of the city came to a bomb damage site, and a natural playground for children, and, especially where there were the remains of a sofa, courting couples. In those days, any snogging or more advanced fumblings had to be done in the open and usually under the cover of darkness.

Named for a lock gate system on the old and long abandoned Arundel - Portsmouth Canal, Locksway Road led to the wild stretches of mudflats and marshland, a row of old shacks and sheds, the Milton piggeries and St James's Hospital. Once a smallpox hospital and sanitorium, St James's went on to specialise in patients with long-term mental health issues. In Victorian times it was known as an Asylum. To us it was the Loony Bin.

A poorhouse in the 17th century, St James's became a 'foundling hospital' early in the next century. This was not a hospital as we would know it, but an 'establishment for the education and maintenance of exposed and deserted young children.' A number of famous philanthropists served on the board of governors, including Jonathan (Gulliver's Travels) Swift and the original Arthur Guinness of the brewing dynasty.

To young boys like us, the Loony Bin was an irresistible challenge, and we would sneak through the gates after dark just for the thrill of an attack by a mad axe man or the local equivalent of Sweeney Todd. Inside, we would peer through windows in the hope of seeing a real loony, or hearing the ghastly screams and cries of the more disturbed inmates. It was local legend that the awful, almost maniacal guffaws of the Laughing Sailor in the machine at Southsea funfair was actually a recording made in the Loony Bin.

Along from the hospital and next to the odiferous Piggeries was the row of shacks of spare timber and corrugated iron which were the equivalent of holiday or weekend cottages for local people, though some were unofficial but permanent residences.

The end of our journey came at the houseboat 'village', a collection of rickety dwellings surrounded the remains of the old lock gates.

It was here we kept our secret stash of cigarettes. Just above high tide mark and in an old metal cash box hidden under a chunk of concrete was the packet of two Player's Weights and a box of matches. It was too risky to hide the evidence at home, as perversely, while smoking was legal and actively encouraged in advertisements, anyone under the age of sixteen would be in real trouble at home or in the street if caught puffing on a fag.

When the coast was clear, we would light up one cigarette and pass it round, trying not to cough and pretending we were enjoying it.

While we smoked and coughed, we would exchange risqué jokes and what we had heard about girls and their strange bits, and discuss what we would do if someone tipped off the police and they arrived to arrest us for under-age smoking.

Bobby said he would swim across to Hayling Island and hide out in the sand dunes until the heat was off. Mike liked my idea of stealing one of the boats moored just offshore and sailing to France and a new life. As it happened, the local CID had other crimes to investigate, so our escape plans were never put into action.

~

Christmas was in the air, and business at the shop more than brisk. With post-war life still austere, Christmas was a big deal and people made the most of the chance to indulge themselves. Our idea of two days of feasting and fun would seem very tame to the average family nowadays, but to us it was something to be enjoyed to the full.

Kay's Store would play a part of in the preparations, and Mother had started a Christmas Club as soon as the shop opened. It was a lot of bother to take tanners and keep a record of who had paid what in to their pot, she said, but it got people into the habit of using the shop. She would also make sure they spent most of their pay out on buying exotic seasonal items like crackers, tins of biscuits, cheese footballs and Marmite twiglets. Technically, the members could take and spend their savings anywhere, but few would get out of the door with their pot intact. In matters of parting customers from their money Mother had, as we used to say, more front than Woolworth, but as the regulars knew, she had been through her own hard times and knew what it was like to be hungry.

In all, it's true to say that in a surprisingly short time we had become a part of the daily lives of hundreds of people in the immediate area. 'Community' is a word which has almost lost its original meaning after being applied to any group with a common interest or persuasion, but in those days, it meant the people who lived down your street and a bit beyond. Like it or not, it was felt to be a duty to keep an eye on and help out old and vulnerable neighbours.

Like a local pub, the corner shop was truly at the

heart of our little community; a place where gossip and rumours as well as useful information was passed on.

As well as shopping, some customers would come in just for a chat, or to try and build up credit, or as we said, put their purchases on the slate. There were no bank accounts for ordinary people, no cheque books and certainly no credit cards. Drinks in the local and groceries were on a cash-only basis, so getting food and fags on tick when the weekly housekeeping ran out was vital. Posh people called it having an 'account': to the rest of us it was having a bit of tick on the slate. My mother was very fussy about who she would trust till payday, while my Celtic big-hearted dad was seen as a soft touch. In truth, she was nowhere near as tough as she liked to pretend, and I know she quietly helped out poor families when they had no food or money to pay for it at the end of the week. She never told dad about her largesse, because, as she said, it would set a bad example...

The shop also played its part in family affairs and occasional dramas. A coin tapping on the window after closing time at eight o clock was a familiar sound, and meant someone had run out of sugar or bread or margarine, or that there was a family emergency. Our telephone was one of less than a handful in the road, and the nearest phone box a good half mile away. In the case of an accident, a burst pipe or a baby on the way, we would be the first to know and be seen as a place to turn to for help. There were even times when my giant of a dad was called in to restrain a drunk and violent husband.

So, there was little that happened in customerland that did not come first or second-hand to Kay's Stores. For good or ill, people knew what the rest of the community was getting up to and disapproval was a useful brake on some otherwise bad behaviour.

Nowadays, people often don't know their immediate neighbours let alone what is happening in their lives, and I'm not sure that's always an improvement.

A popular science-fantasy story of the 1950s has two strangers sitting in a bar. One asks the other, who is smoking, for a light. He says 'no' and the rebuffed man asks why. 'If I give you a light,' says the smoker with a half-smile, 'you'll buy me a drink and then I will feel bound to return the compliment. We'll inevitably get talking and stay on far longer and drink much more than we intended. If we get home safely, we will be in trouble with our wives, and divorce or worse could follow. By giving you a light, I could change both our lives...and not necessarily for the better.' Regardless, the stranger does give the man a light, and his prediction that their lives will change dramatically is proved chillingly correct.

I repeat that philosophical tale because, whether you believe in self-determination or everything being down to Kismet or fate, I think it would be true to say that even small choices can change the course of our lives significantly. Like most people with many more years behind them than to come, I made lots of choices. Some have turned out to have been good ones, some not so clever, and some verging on lunacy.

My first life-changing decision had come when my parents opened the envelope containing the results of my performance in the 11-plus examinations.

I had done well, Mother said the letter said. In fact, I had done very well in spite of my indifference to paying attention at Cottage Grove. In those days, pupils were offered a place in secondary schools based on the results of the 11-plus. Unfair, perhaps, to presume a child was best suited to become a doctor or architect, plumber or labourer on the basis of a single examination, but that was how it was. In the three-tier system, those who had done best were offered a place at a grammar school. Those in the middle ranking were offered a school majoring in crafts, while 'secondary moderns' were the no-option option for the rest.

So well had I done that I was invited take a place at one of the two city grammar schools. Almost as an afterthought, the letter said that if a grammar-school education did not suit my parents' plans for my future, I would be welcome at the Portsmouth Technical High School.

I shall not forget my poor mother's face when I said I did not want to go to a grammar school; I wanted to be like brother John, who had gone to the Building School and already signed up for an apprenticeship as a pipe fitter and welder.

All that afternoon my mother tried to persuade me to at least consider going to the local grammar, but as ever she let me have my way.

I often think how differently my life would have turned out had I gone for academia rather than pipe strangling. For sure, as the man in the pub said, my life would have been very different. And, as my wife says whenever I moan about missed chances, I could have been run over by a bus on my way to my first week at Portsmouth Grammar School.

~

It was about now that the proprietors of Kay's Stores gained further social status.

As well as a telephone, we became the second family in Frensham Road to own a motor car, the other plutocrat being the greengrocer next door.

Our set of wheels was a pre-war Vauxhall 14 and looked as if it had been in the wars and fallen on hard times. Dents and tears were copious, and rust had feasted on the bodywork. The dents were easily knocked out with a ball-peen hammer, and I remember helping dad give Tin Lizzie an all-over paint job. He'd done a deal with a Dockyard worker and given him a packet of Woodbines for a tin of the viscous bright red paint the man said they used to make submarines waterproof. We sloshed it on with the wide, dockyard-issue 'toshing' brushes the man had supplied for another packet of fags, and it certainly held the rust together and made Tin Lizzie stand out. The originally chromium-plated flukes running along each side of the bonnet were picked out with the leftovers of the custard yellow paint dad had used on the shop-front. Our tarted-up car rarely moved, but in its bright livery would sit outside the shop as a symbol of the family's success and status.

Like all shops of any size and most businesses, Kay's Stores was shut on Sundays, and that was when Tin Lizzie came into her own. Mother would make fish paste and jam and sometimes even cheese sandwiches and we would set off for a picnic at Petersfield lake. For a small boy it was quite an adventure to travel the eighteen miles into the heart of the countryside where grass was more common than pavements. On the way back we would stop off for a pint or two of watery mild ale for dad, and a cherry brandy for Mother. Not that exciting as a family outing nowadays, perhaps, but in 1954 it seemed we lived as gods on that precious day.

~

Christmas Eve, and Bobby and Mike and I are standing outside Milton Library. Between us, we've borrowed enough books to see us through the holidays, and almost cleared the shelves of *Billy Bunter, Jennings Goes to School* and the *Just William* series.

Soon, we'll club together to buy two fish cakes, a saveloy, a polony and two large helpings of chips for a pre-Christmas orgy on the bowling club verandah. Now, dusk is settling on the frost and moonshiney rooftops as we look up at the starry sky and scent the crisp, sharp air in anticipation of what is to come. This particular evening will become one of my most precious childhood memories. It had been a year of change, with leaving my old home and friends and haunts, and more change lying ahead with my first term at a new school. But young enough to adapt to change and find it exciting, and I knew that whatever was to come, I had a better and happier life than so many children of my age in post-war Britain. Despite what we might like to say, Bobby, Mike and I knew how lucky we were to have been born during the War and not have had to leave home and fight in it, and perhaps not return.

1955

~ Ruth Ellis becomes the last woman to hang in the UK

~ Stirling Moss is the first English driver to win the British Grand Prix

~ Princes Margaret announces she does not intend marrying the divorced Group Captain Peter Townsend

~ The first Guinness Book of records is published

~ 77 people lose their lives in the Le Mans 24-Hour Race disaster

~ Apartheid is under way in South Africa, and 60,000 non-white residents of a Johannesburg suburb are forcibly evicted

~ The first Disneyland resort and theme park is opened in California

~ Winston Churchill resigns as prime minister due to ill-health at the age of 80

~ Christopher Cockerell patents his design for a hovercraft

~ The population of the world is declared at 2,755,823,000

~ Members of the Pompey soccer team visit the Conservative Club in Fratton Road, where they are entertained by Mrs Gwen Miller on piano and Mr G Watts on drums.

Top Tunes

Mystery Train ~ Elvis Presley
I can't tell a Waltz from a Tango ~ Alma Cogan
Cherry Pink and Apple Blossom White ~ Eddie
Calvert
Let Me Go, Lover ~ *Dean Martin* and *Ruby Murray*
Rock Around the Clock ~ Bill Hayley and his
Comets
The Yellow Rose of Texas ~ Mich Miller
Unchained Melody ~ Jimmy Young
The Ballad of Davey Crocket ~ Bill Hayes
Love is a Many Splendoured Thing ~ The Four Aces
Sixteen Tons ~ Tennessee Ernie Ford
Ain't that a Shame ~ Pat Boone
Mr Sandman ~ Dickie Valentine
The Naughty Lady of Shady Lane ~ The Ames
Brothers
Under the Bridges of Paris ~ Dean Martin with
Eartha Kitt
Hey There ~ Johnny Ray and Rosemary Clooney

Put your glad rags on and join me hon'
We'll have some fun when the clock strikes one
We're gonna rock around the clock tonight
We're gonna rock, rock, rock, 'till broad daylight
We're gonna rock, gonna rock around the clock
tonight

Rock around the Clock by Bill Hayley and the
Comets - Lyrics by James E. Myers & Max C.
Freedman

My first week at my new school, and I'd already had a painful encounter with Gus Gates and his infamous cane. It would not be my last. Afterwards, I was told by the older boys that the red weal across my left palm was quite a status symbol, though I would rather have done without it.

Seen from the front, Portsmouth Technical High School looked quite impressive. A school since 1905, the solid redbrick building sat behind a tall hedge, with double gates leading to a flight of steps to the grandly arched entrance. Behind and beyond this imposing façade, the place looked like a badly-maintained army transit camp.

On the solid side to and behind the main building stood a shabby, single-storey building where school dinners were served. It was also used for assemblies or special events like torturing new boys. The building overlooked the playing field, which I remember was maintained by a strange character who would nowadays have been arrested if he came within a hundred yards of any school gate. Mind you, now I think of it, some of the teachers would fall into that category.

Beyond the playing field was what looked like the set for a World War II prisoner-of-war film. The row of wooden huts had been built to accommodate American troops as they waited for the off for D-Day, and now used as classrooms.

Nearby, the big and permanently odiferous toilet block was of the same vintage as the huts, and apart from its official purpose was also used for fights, swapping porno stories and drawings, and a torture room for new boys when the dining hall was occupied.

~

I'd arrived for my first day on the school bus, feeling stiff and uncomfortable in my new uniform. Mother had taken me to the Co-op for my blazer (36 shillings and sixpence all sizes) and short trousers at twenty-seven and sixpence. After my casual school dress at Cottage Grove, it was like wearing a badly-fitting suit of armour. Worse of all was the cap. It was the largest in the outfitters but still looked, as my dad observed, like a pimple of a Dutch cheese. I kept my cap in my pocket on the bus, but forgot Bobby Harrigan's warning to put it on and do my tie up before arriving at the school gate. I was soon to pay the painful price for ignoring his advice.

My future nemesis and the first teacher I met looked exactly how one would imagine the Devil would appear if he had thinly disguised himself while wandering around on earth looking for new recruits. At first sight, the Deputy Head Master put me in mind of the markings on the back of a death's head moth. 'Gus' Gates had a skull-like face, the skin straining across his high cheek bones and emphasising his deep-set eyes. To me, they seemed to smoulder and glow like diabolical coals. The Satanic image was enhanced by the way his thick and immaculately-kept white hair was swept back to reveal a widow's peak, and eyebrows slanted like Fu Manchu at his most fiendish. As the years passed, I would realise he was a fair and even good man with the school and pupils at the heart of his concerns. He just believed in law and order. and his core belief was obviously that discipline was the key to ensuring we left school best equipped to face what the world had to throw at us. For sure he was sure that to spare the rod was to spoil the child.

One of his ways of enforcing the rules was to hide behind a tree alongside the main gate and lay in wait for boys who arrived improperly dressed. The one I had fallen foul of was that caps had to be worn at all times on the way to or from school.

The sentence for breaking this rule or having a tie askew or even a jacket unbuttoned was one stroke of the cane. And that was just for the first offence. Further transgressions would result in what was ironically referred to as 'two of the best'. Today's pupils - sorry 'students' - may find it hard to believe that corporal punishment was the norm in those days. Some teachers like our gentle chemistry teacher clearly abhorred the idea of physical aggression, while others like Mr Gates believed it was a necessary corrective. At the far end of the scale, there were teachers who actually enjoyed inflicting pain. I can recall only one genuine sadist at the Technical High, but more of him later.

~

As well as the change of home and school, I now found some disturbing things happening to my body. Suddenly, just lying in bed would feel like I was on a rack, which Mother assured me were just 'growing pains'. Other strange changes were those I could not ask her about and she chose not to mention. One was how hairs had started to sprout around my willy. It was also developing a mind of its own, and something lumpy was growing directly below my little mushroom. At least I was spared the agony of some boys at school who suddenly seemed to be growing breasts. They were not just excess fat, but proper, pointy little boobs. I can't imagine the mental torment to whom it happened, and it wasn't helped by merciless teasing from those who didn't get an overload of oestrogen. I know some sufferers invented verrucas or came up with other excuses to avoid swimming or using the changing rooms, and they got little sympathy from the teaching staff.

It's another hard-to-believe fact for people born less than fifty years ago that in those more buttoned-up times is that there was no official information about sex and reproduction and all the weird things happening to our bodies as puberty struck.

Unlike nowadays when there often seems an overload of information, nobody thought of telling us about what was coyly referred to as The Birds and Bees. This meant we got our information from older boys, which inevitably led to confusion, error and even terror.

I remember a boy from the second year telling me and a horrified bunch of first-formers how girls started to bleed into their pants every month when they reached a certain age. This was, he said, because they had teeth in their fannies which had to be removed before they could 'do it' with boys and risk causing him serious damage.

~

Meanwhile, we new boys were getting to know the men charged with guiding us to, as the school song had it, Manhood's Verge.

They were a varied bunch, and some seemed eccentric or unsettled in their roles. This may have been because they would have fought in and survived the War. Certainly, I can't remember any of them talking about those dark years or what they did then.

For pupils, members of the teaching staff were generally divided into the good, bad and worse. Classification would be affected by whether you liked the subject the teacher taught, and of course whether he liked you.

One of my favourites was Basher Humby, and I think that was mostly because he was easily steered away from actually teaching us anything. Geography was his subject, although his interest and knowledge of countries seemed limited to those coloured pink on the map of the world on the classroom wall. It was well out of date and from a time when the sun truly never set on the British Empire, and that was how Basher liked it.

I remember him as a gnome-like, wizened figure

who seemed well beyond retirement age and who would have been in his prime in the Victorian era. He was the kindest and most gentle of men, and got his name from the practice of bashing his walking stick on a nearby desk to call the class to order.

The trick for getting out of formal lessons was to ask Basher an apparently innocent question about the Middle East, then sit back and pretend to listen to his memoirs.

In fact, his tales of adventuring in faraway lands were always of interest. I once asked him in jest if he had known Lawrence of Arabia, and it turned out he had.

"Come everyone and let's rejoice
And sing this song with heart and voice,
And praise the school that leads the way
To manhood's verge from boyhood state
And helps us meet the chance of fate.
So let us sing with voices full
The praises of our honoured school"

-Portsmouth Technical High School Song
(to the best of my memory)

1956

- ~ Test Pilot Peter Twiss becomes the first man to fly at more than 1000 mph
- ~ Premium Bonds are launched, with a draw for a top prize of £1000
- ~ The 2 i's coffee bar, launchpad for the skiffle boom, Cliff Richard and Tommy Steele opens in London
- ~ Egyptian leader Gamal Nasser announces the 'nationalisation' of the Suez Canal, triggering the Suez Crisis
- ~ Ridden by future best-selling author Dick Francis, the Queen Mother's horse Devon Lock mysteriously collapses yards from the finishing post in the Grand National
- ~ The possession of heroin becomes fully criminalised
- ~ Humphrey Lyttelton and his band record Bad Penny Blues, the first jazz record to enter the UK charts
- ~ Working for MI6, frogman Lionel 'Buster' Crabb dives secretly in Portsmouth Harbour to investigate a Russian warship and is never seen again.

Top Tunes

The Girl Can't Help It ~ *Little Richard*
See You Later, Alligator ~ Bill Hayley and his
Comets
Heart break Hotel ~ Elvis Presley
Bad Penny Blues ~ Humphrey Lyttelton
The Poor People of Paris ~ Winifred Attwell
Why do Fools fall in Love ~ Frankie Lymon and the
Teenagers
Lay Down your Arms ~ Anne Shelton
Rock and Roll Waltz ~ Kay Starr
Just Walkin' in the Rain ~ Johnny Ray
Green Door ~ Frankie Vaughan
The Great Pretender ~ The Platters
Hot Diggity Dog ~ Perry Como

The girl can't help it, she was born to please,
She can't help it, the girl can't help it,
And if she's got, a figure made to squeeze,
She can't help it, the girl can't help it,
Won't you kindly be aware, the girl can't help it,
The girl can't help it,
If she mesmerizes, every mother's son,
She can't help it, the girl can't help it,

The Girl Can't Help It by Little Richard. Lyrics and music by Bobby Troup

A new year and, after a lot of attention and hard work, my Elvis quiff was looking good.

In a sort of reverse exponential ratio, as it grew slicker and shinier and more bounteous, my educative rating slid correspondingly downhill. Due to a lack of attention in lessons and a growing interest in girls, pop music and my hair, I had been demoted from the 'A' to the 'B' stream. Luckily and as far as I can remember, that was as low as you could go.

Apart from disappointment for Mother, this meant losing French lessons - which I liked - and having to choose between making a badly sugar-twisted poker in Metalwork or a wonky pipe rack in Woodwork. Another of my bad choices came when I opted for the metalwork course because I thought it more manly than messing around with a sheet of sandpaper.

This surprisingly common male desire to look, as we said, 'hard' and cool even affected my morning cycle to school.

Once out of sight of the shop, I'd pull over to

loosen and turn the handlebars so they pointed down (forbidden as too dangerous by Mother), stuff my school cap into the pocket of my mac and turn the collar up to give me a dashing air. Then I'd dangle a fake cardboard cigarette from the corner of my mouth, adjust my quiff and set out again. If I passed any promising-looking girls or stroppy-looking boys, I would move my feet so the heels were on the pedals and the toes stuck out almost at right angles. Don't ask me why, but that was the lairy, 'I'm hard' way to ride a bike in those days. Another was to walk with your feet in the same position and arms akimbo, like a cormorant drying its wings. To some males, the pedal position would have been seen as a challenge. To grown-ups and females, it must have looked like the rider had a serious mobility problem with his ankle joints.

~

We were not yet teenagers, and most of my mates didn't have a clue as to what they wanted to do for a living when they left school. Conversely, all the swats seemed to know exactly what they wanted to be and do for the rest of their lives.

The only thing I knew for certain was that I wanted to be famous. I had already worked out that becoming famous would make me rich, and being rich and famous in the right way would provide an endless stream of girlfriends. I was still not sure why or what I wanted the girls for, but they seemed an essential part of what lay ahead.

At first, I thought that an actor's life might be for me. All they did was read out someone else's words and they got very rich and famous. James Dean was an obvious example, and his quiff wasn't a patch on mine. People said I looked a bit like him, so now he was dead I could maybe take his place as a rebel without a cause.

There didn't seem to be many openings for a would-be thespian in Milton, so I thought I'd start off by becoming an actor-manager with my own theatre. Within a week I'd written a play about the Storming of the Bastille, hung a pair of curtains up in my bedroom and made some tickets with my John Bull Printing Outfit.

Ticket sales were not good; in fact, they were all complimentary and the only takers were Bobby Harrigan, Mick Beacon and Dougie Cooper, a budding entrepreneur whose style and cheek I admired. He would stage summer fetes in his backyard and charge visitors threepence for entry. An additional charge of a penny would be made for catching a rat made of a couple of old socks before it emerged from a piece of drainpipe tubing, or throwing a tennis ball at a line of kindling wood sitting on the garden wall. The prize for catching the rat or knocking over all the sticks was an orange nicked from Mr Weekes' shop front display, or a tube of sweets I suspect was nicked from Kay's Stores. I never saw anyone knock over all the kindling sticks, and later found several had been glued to the board on which they sat.

The opening performance of Death to The Aristos was also its closing performance, and as I played all the characters, I was not sorry to take the curtains down and put a career as an actor on hold.

~

I realised we were going up in the world when I arrived home after school to see a small box sitting in the corner of the back room. Televisions with a pay-as-you-view coin box on the side were becoming popular, but Mother had bought the almost brand new 14-inch BushTV53 outright. The screen was not much bigger than a modest electronic tablet, but to us and millions of Britons it was the wonder of the age.

The BBC's broadcasting hours were limited to between 9am and 11pm. There were no programmes between six and seven 'o' clock, which was to allow parents get the kids to bed before settling down for an evening's viewing. Popular light entertainment programmes included Take Your Pick with Michael Miles bullying the entrants into choosing a box to open and win a substantial prize or a leaky balloon. Hosted by the ever-affable Eamonn Andrews, What's My Line featured a panel of TV personalities like Lady Isobel Barnet and the dependably irascible Gilbert Harding figuring out the unusual occupations of studio guests based on their brief mimes. Other popular programmes were Dixon of Dock Green, Opportunity Knocks and The Adventures of Sir Lancelot. When TV sets became common, pubs would be virtually empty on the night Hancock's Half Hour was broadcast.

~

The lack of tv sets in the area meant some of our customers would ask to share ours. When the shop had opened, people would ask to use the phone; now they asked if they could sit in and watch a programme they liked the look of. Some even began taking The Radio Times so they could make their selection for the week's viewing.

My dad was happy to share viewing, but ever the entrepreneur, my mother considered setting up a pay-per-view scheme. She settled for buying a handful of used sets at auction, and Kay's TV Rentals was born. The idea was that the customers would pay a half a crown a week, and dad would be on hand to fix them in the case of a problem. The scheme never really got off the ground, and was scrapped when Mother noticed that the pretty young widow at number 16 and the landlady of the Devonshire Arms seemed to have an inordinate amount of breakdowns.

~

If the weather was bad, I would leave the bike at home and take the school bus. It meant wearing the dreaded pimple-on-a-Dutch-cheese cap, but the upside was that I could spend the journey time doing the homework due in that morning. We were supposed to spend ninety minutes each evening, studying, revising and doing the homework tasks set for that day. This of course was a ridiculous expectation for a healthy 12-year-old. There was my social life with a growing bunch of friends, comics to read and at least half an hour working on my quiff. The solution was to persuade one of the swots in my class to let me copy his submissions in exchange for sweets, pretend friendship or, if necessary, the offer of protection.

I soon learned that verbatim copying of essays and

answers was a mistake and easily spotted by the teacher. Depending on the level of transgression or the mood of the teacher, this could mean anything from 'I must not cheat' lines to extra homework, detention or even physical retribution. I preferred the fleeting pain of a stroke or two of the cane rather than the other sanctions, and the number of strokes I accumulated over the term put me in contention for the annual Most Caned Award.

~

Though I'd always thought of myself as a Southsea boy, moving to Milton was almost like returning to the family roots. Dad's mother and stepfather had lived in Glasgow Road before the War and were now running The Three Marines pub in Eastney. In those days it was hard to make a living from a corner local, and grandfather East would go to work in the dockyard during the day after sorting out the barrels and bottles in the cellar and bar. Grandma Kelly would make her regal appearance each evening, sweeping down the stairs and into the lounge bar, acknowledging favoured regulars and ignoring those who were just visiting or those she thought of as public bar material. Naturally, she never went into the Public, but could quell a noisy customer from fifty foot away with a glacial glare.

A few hundred yards from the pub, Mother had been born above the two shops her grandfather had set up after leaving the Royal Marines. One sold cold meats, pease pudding and pies. In the other, he bought clothes from conscripts arriving at nearby Eastney Barracks, then sold them to those leaving the service. It's probably where Mother got her flair for business and seeing a market. As she used to say in only a half-joking manner, her worst deal was falling in love with and marrying the gangling figure wearing a grubby raincoat, standing outside her bedsitter with a mangy greyhound on the end of a piece of string.

~

Another milestone on the road to adulthood.

Returning aflame with images and ideas of how life could be from the Paris exchange trip, I found my dreams pervaded by nightly visits from the Sex Kitten. Brigitte would leave her poster on the dormitory wall and come to my bedside most nights. She did nothing more than stand at the foot of the bed pouting, but it was enough to make my little willy grow much bigger. Some mornings I would wake up with a sticky front to my pyjama bottoms. I didn't know what it was, and worried that I was leaking my life fluids, which in a way I suppose I was.

1957

- 'Asian flu' arrives in the UK, where it will kill between 20-30,000 people
- Paul McCartney meets future fellow Beatle John Lennon when Lennon's skiffle group play at a Liverpool garden fete
- Stanley Matthews plays his final international soccer game for England
- A report by the Medical Research Council announces it has found a link between smoking and lung cancer
- Norwich City Council becomes the first local authority to install a computer
- The Cavern Club opens in Liverpool as a venue for jazz fans
- Windscale nuclear reactor catches fire and releases radioactive contamination
- The first successful testing of a British Hydrogen bomb takes place at The Christmas Isles in the Pacific
- Cricketer David Gower, darts genius Eric Bristow and comedienne Jo Brand are born

Top Tunes

(Let me be Your) Teddy Bear ~ Elvis Presley
All Shook Up ~ Elvis Presley
That'll be the Day ~ Buddy Holly and the Crickets
Diana ~ Paul Anka
Love Letters in the Sand ~ Pat Boone
Young Love ~ Tab Hunter
Little Darlin' ~ The Diamonds
Great Balls of Fire ~ Jerry 'Killer' Lee Lewis
Cumberland Gap ~ Lonnie Donegan and The Vipers
skiffle group
Don't You Rock Me, Daddy-O ~ Lonnie Donegan
and The Vipers
Singing The Blues ~ Tommy Steele and The
Steelmen, Guy Mitchell
Wake Up, Little Susie ~ The Everly Brothers
Lucille ~ Little Richard
The Garden of Eden ~ Frankie Vaughan
The Banana Boat Song ~ Harry Belafonte

A well'a bless my soul
What'sa wrong with me?
I'm itchin' like a man in a fuzzy tree
My friends say I'm actin' wild as a bug
I'm in love
I'm all shook up

All Shook Up by Elvis Presley. Lyrics by Otis Blackwell

The new year brought more change and with its arrival I became a teenager.

My entry to the time of fierce joys, deep sorrows and unreasoning anger were not signalled by dramatic changes. My voice had already broken and the growing pains had stopped. I had been spared the ordeal of sprouting boy breasts, my testes were behaving themselves, but something nasty had arrived on the back of my neck. Mother diagnosed acne and dismissed it as a rite of passage for most young people. I could but wonder if some of my mates were right, and the angry red spots had appeared because I was by now a practised hand at masturbation.

On a positive note, I now knew exactly what I wanted to do when I left school.

A strident example of what was to become known as the Youth Revolution was the revolution in the music charts. In the early Fifties, crooners and female 'torch singers' with their soppy songs ruled the airwaves. Now, the stage belonged to the next generation, and we liked our music loud, in-your-face and all our own. In 1954, the film *Blackboard*

Jungle had featured Bill Hayley's *Rock around the Clock,* giving teddy boys the excuse to slash a lot of cinema seats. Then came the tidal wave of American rock 'n' rollers and their instant imitators this side of the Atlantic. At the same time, skiffle had arrived in the UK and Lonnie Donegan was, in some quarters, more popular than Elvis Presley. The climax for me (in more ways than one) came with the ultimate rock 'n' roll movie.

The Girl Can't Help it hit our screens in 1956, and starred the pneumatic and, to me, highly underrated Jayne Mansfield. Almost more importantly, it featured a host of rock and roll greats singing their most memorable hits. Watching Eddie Cochran appearing on stage to tumultuous applause to sing Twenty Flight Rock and Little Richard with his monumental pompadour hairstyle and shiny suit of lights belting out Reddy Teddy literally made my knees go weak. All that and Ms. Mansfield as well. What more could a randy young rock fan want?

I now understood exactly what I needed to do to become rich and famous and have an unending supply of sexy ladies throwing themselves at my feet. Sod the acting, I would become a Pop Star.

I had no guitar let alone the ability to play one and couldn't carry a note, but that seemed no handicap. One sort of pop music used household and everyday object for their instruments, and so the Milton Skiffle Kings were born. It wasn't rock 'n' roll, but it would do for a start.

~

Back in the real world, I continued to live on the

edge at school, cheating with my homework and doing just enough to avoid expulsion as a hopeless case. I think one of the reasons I received more than what I thought my fair share of punishment was because the teachers knew I was bright enough to do well if I could be bothered. I just couldn't be arsed with learning about logarithms, sines and cosines and the Repeal of the Corn Laws when there was my quiff to work on or the adventures of The Deathless Men to keep up with in the Wizard comic. This made some teachers angry, and they would take it out on me, sometimes physically.

In particular, one master would nowadays have been branded as a sadist and doubtless done jail time. He was a burly, beefy man with a pudding-like face and a mini-quiff, and his proud boast was that he could lift any boy clean off his feet with a swipe to the backside from his size 12 plimsolls. As I was the heaviest boy in the class, I was often used to prove his claim.

Some years after leaving school, I met my old tormentor in the street. I was on my way to the pub and I could see that he recognised me as we drew level. 'Hello sir,' I said. 'Hello, er, East,' he replied and hurried on. It seemed to me he had fear in his eyes. I paused and thought about all the times I had promised myself revenge, then shrugged and walked on to the pub.

~

Thanks to scrounging and a touch of ingenuity, the Milton Skiffle Kings were tooled up and ready to go. Mick Beacon was on washboard, not by inclination but because his mum had one. This meant we could practise every day of the week except Monday, which was washday regardless of the weather. He had also borrowed two thimbles from his mother's sewing box, and quickly picked up the scrape-and-tap routine.

Bobby Harrigan was on drums, made with empty Quality Street sweet tins from the shop. With a couple of editions of the Portsmouth News cut into circles and taped on the bottom, we liked to think they sounded almost like the real thing. Bobby started with kindling wood as drumsticks, but then got a proper pair when his parents noticed the splinters and took pity on him.

I played, to use the word loosely, what was known as tea chest bass. This comprised the wooden sounding-box with a length of string running from it up to a nail at the top of a broomstick. The bottom of the stick was held against the top of the box, and the string plucked. Different notes were theoretically achieved by the amount of tension put on the string. This was beyond the range of my tin ear, so we settled for the one note. Altogether, we managed a sort of rhythmic, shuffling beat, with me usually slightly behind the pace. Making the most of available materials, it was, I suppose, the forerunner of the voice-only beat-box.

Being tone-deaf and talentless in any aspect of music-making, I was no help with vocals but saw myself as the driving force to break through into the big time. And after endless rehearsals in my room, we believed we were ready for our first gig. Thinking about it, the obvious person to act as our agent, promoter and manager was Dougie Cooper. Then he would be called a trainee spiv; nowadays an embryo 'Del Boy' Trotter.

Our first and last performance was staged in Dougie's front room while his dad was at work and his mum out shopping. He'd made and distributed posters announcing the first appearance of the world-famous Milton Skiffle Kings, but we only attracted an audience of one. Stanley Cooper was a rather delicate, Jewish boy who went to a posh private school in Southsea. He was a trusting soul and agreed to pay the entrance fee of a shilling when Dougie told him that folk star Nancy Whisky* had promised to try and drop in.

As it happened, the string on my tea chest base broke during our version of Cumberland Gap and the washboard was missing because it was a Monday.

Our audience demanded his money back, and we decided that it should be the swansong of the Milton Skiffle Kings. The fact was that none of us went for skiffle. As far as we were concerned, it just wasn't cool and smacked too much of earnest men (and some women) with beards getting excited about whether chewing gum loses its flavour on the bedpost overnight. Rock 'n' Roll was king, and if we were going to dream impossible dreams, it would be of being Just Like Eddie.

*Historical Note: 'Skiffle' had its roots in American jazz blues and folk songs and arrived in Britain in the early 1950s. It was performed with a mixture of household and improvised instruments and many bands and performers (including John Lennon)) started with skiffle songs. Chas McDevitt and Nancy

Whisky reigned as king and queen of the genre for a short while with Freight Train, released in 1956 and reaching number five in the UK charts the following year.

~

As the term dragged by, lessons seemed ever more pointless and no use to a future pop star. Why would I need to know how to work out the volume of a cylinder or the odd prime number when on tour with my rock band? And some of the subjects seemed a complete waste of time. A classic example was Music Appreciation with Bill Blood, or, as we knew him, Old Pocket Billiards.

The weekly sessions took place in one of the large wooden huts lining the far edge of the playing fields. Even by the standards of those days, they were not a suitable setting for absorbing an education. They were smelly, draughty and creaky, stifling in the summer and freezing in the winter. The sole means of heating was a pot-bellied stove, which was the favoured position for the teacher. His toadies would get as close as they could and appear to be hanging on his every word while trying to keep warm. We bad boys would shiver defiantly at the back of the class, and got our revenge by pouring milk on the stove before the lessons started. It made a revolting smell, even compared to the toilet block and some of the rank odours created in Chemistry.

Bill Blood seemed a decent if dour and generally uncommunicative man, and not one to enthuse a pupil to follow or take up a career in classical music. A typical session would start with him announcing the movement, symphony or work, then explaining in detail the meaning of the piece and who played what. It was not enough to have to sit through Peter and the Wolf; we had to appreciate that Peter was represented by the string section, his grandfather by the bassoon and the Big Bad Wolf by the French horn.

Then the needle would be dropped into the groove of the ancient gramophone and Mr Blood would enter a trance-like state while conducting vigorously with one hand, while the other fiddled endlessly with coins or keys or whatever was in his left-hand pocket. That, of course, was where his nickname had come from.

~

Inevitably and in spite of protestations of eternal friendship, I had gradually lost contact with my chums from Castle Road and Cottage Grove. But I had my new mates in Milton and at school.

I've never been able to make out why or how we choose our friends, but in my case, it certainly can't be because of similarities in temperament or interests. In later years I followed the practice of having lots of disparate acquaintances and a few true friends, randomly selected from people of all origins, classes and wealth levels, and this happenstance had its roots at The Tech. I knew a hundred or so boys on nodding terms, but had no more than a handful of real mates. After initial forays and engagements, I would conclude that girls could never be proper friends.

Two of my best classmate-mates were Michael

Marshall and Dave Burgess. Like my childhood chums in Castle Road, Mike's dad was a Naval Officer and his mum a suitably refined lady.

Like my family. Dave came from solid, respectable working-class stock, He was a sturdy and steady, even stoical chap who sometimes bore a slightly worried look as if he suspected trouble might be on the horizon. This was probably because he spent so much of his spare time with me. I think our opposing attitudes complemented each other, and for whatever reason, our friendship endured. He ended up as a police sergeant in a Hampshire village location, and I sometimes wonder if his time with me was the spur to join the forces of law and order.

From our first year together in 2b, Dave would arrive with his rolled-up towel every Saturday morning. If we had to pay (it was hard to avoid or deceive conductors in those days), we would spend a halfpenny on the bus fare to the town centre and the City Baths. This was an almost impossible place to bunk into, which made it an irresistible challenge.

As well as an official verruca plague centre, the City Baths was a riotously noisy place on Saturday mornings, filled with boys showing off by bombing girls or jumping on mates from the highest diving board. Sometimes blood would tinge the water, but I don't recall any serious accidents or deaths by drowning.

Apart from the odd Lascar seaman or West Indian resident, Portsmouth was a very white place then. I remember once seeing a black boy at the baths and the attention he got. I know racism was rife in those times, but there were so few black or brown people in the city that it was a real curiosity to see someone of such a different colour and appearance. The little boy was stared at and even stroked like some exotic animal, but I don't remember any aggression. As far as most kids I knew were concerned, a gollywog was no more than a doll. Most seen on a jar of marmalade. 'Nigger' was Dam Buster hero Guy Gibson's dog or a shade of popular shoe polish. My best mate and sparring partner after leaving school was black. He didn't seem to be on the receiving end of a lot of racist remarks or behaviour, but perhaps that was because he had such a good right hook.

After the swim, Dave and I would sneak down the alley next door and climb on to the window ledge of the city mortuary in the hope of seeing a dead body or bits of one. We never saw anything out of the ordinary, but there was a chilling air about the building and a smell of formaldehyde which seemed overpowering even though it was probably just our imagination.

Next in our Saturday morning routine was the superb ice cream parlour in the Guildhall square. Smells can stay longest and strongest in the memory, and at Verrecchias a fragrance of freshly ground coffee and vanilla ice cream hung in the air and seemed to come away with you. We would eat our threepenny cones leaning on the railings above the road running beneath the railway bridge, then take a stroll in the park to stare in wonder at proper tramps and do our best to make courting couples feel uncomfortable.

It was at one of these Saturday morning swimming sessions that a bigger boy taught me how to make my willy go hard on purpose. He demonstrated how it was done in a cubicle, and said that if I kept at it long enough it would shoot something called spunk out of the end. It felt really good, he said, but when you were new to it you had to be careful. Overdoing it could give you a really bad headache and might even make your balls explode.

He was right about the headache, which I found to be similar to eating a Verrecchia ice cream too quickly. After only one mostly-successful attempt I decided to wait till I was older and more able, as it were, to handle it better. It seemed to me that my willy was quite fit for purpose at its normal size, and I certainly did not want to make my balls any bigger, or lose them in some sort of dreadful and incendiary act of a Vengeful God.

~

After years of standing outside a pub with a packet of crisps, a straw and a dumpy bottle of lemonade, I was to make my first crossing of the threshold as a customer. The action would be re-enacted thousands of times in coming years, but, as with sex, that first time remains a very special memory.

It was close to opening time; the streetlights were reflected brightly in the wet pavements and we were standing under the awning of a shop near Fratton Park. I remember clearly feeling at the same time excited and very nervous. Again, like the first time I had sex.

I forget whose idea it was, but we had decided to try and get served in one of the local boozers. So close to Fratton Park, we were spoiled for choice. There were four pubs within yards of each other, and unusually for Portsmouth, three were owned by different brewery companies.

Nearest to the ground was Whitbread's Cremorne Gardens, and across the road stood The Traveller's Joy, one of only a handful of Friary Meux pubs in the city. On one corner of Priory Crescent was The Brewer's Arms, owned by local brewer Gales, and on the other side of the road stood The Milton Arms.

Milton park was part of what had been a farm, and the Milton Arms had been home to farmer Goldsmith, for whom a nearby avenue was named. Apparently original but probably enhanced, the pub had a traditional Olde Worlde beam and plaster frontage, and in the yard behind was a ricketty-racketty building known as The Barn Bar. This, we decided, would be the best place to try and get served our first drink on licenced premises.

In those days, public houses were often known by the name of the landlord, especially if he was a bit of a character. The tradition would persist even after the departure or death of the landlord. So, The pub opposite Bransbury park on the borders of Eastney was not The Cumberland Tavern to the majority of its regular users. It was Charlie Hurdle's. Across the road, the Fort Cumberland was more popularly known as Pavey's. And so, sometimes long-dead landlords were immortalised.

The Milton Arms was known to locals as Probert's, and we knew that the Barn bar was usually tended by an elderly man known to locals as Old Bob, and rumoured to be in a relationship with the widowed landlady. Mike had done some research, and we knew that Old Bob was very short-sighted and fond of a drink, and only got off his stool behind the bar to serve. The lighting was also usually low.

At the gate to the yard, hearts beating as we tried to look unconcerned, we went through our plan of action. At fourteen, Bobby was the oldest and by far the tallest, so he would be our front man. A couple of pub customs, he said, were that ladies never bought drinks for themselves or anyone else, while groups of men usually used a system called the 'round'. That meant they took it in turns to pay for each other's drinks. Bobby's dad said it could cause a lot of animosity if someone didn't buy himself one when it was his round, but it was an old pub tradition. So, we would pool our funds and he would do the ordering.

Accordingly, we each contributed to a pot totalling one-and-sixpence. Another ploy, Bobby said, would be to ask for three 'small' beers rather than halves, as that is what really regular pubgoers did. With his short-back-and sides and round, fresh face, Mike looked the youngest of us, so he should go straight to the table furthest from the bar, preferably in a corner and nowhere near a light. I would accompany Bobby to the bar to help with the drinks.

We had no watches to synchronise, but felt like a group of soldiers making ready to depart on a dangerous mission. We didn't actually shake hands, but took deep breaths, wished ourselves good luck, braced our shoulders and walked towards the bar.

~

After practising a casual expression, turning up the collar of his raincoat and warning Mike to take off his school cap, Bobby led the way in.

It was truly gloomy inside, more than probably a money-saving rather than mood-creating policy. As our eyes got used to the dark, we saw a balding, large-bellied old man, sitting on a bar stool behind the counter. He did not look up as we approached, and appeared to be dozing or deep in reverie, possibly thinking of his lost youth, or perhaps his next drink.

'Evening, guv'nor,' said Bobby gruffly. '… I'll take three small black beers.'

There was no response, and we held our breaths as the old man looked up and at us through heavily veined eyes. I was sure he must be able to hear the wild thumping of my heart, and even in the gloom, Mike looked like a schoolboy without his cap on. The old man sighed, then reached up and scratched his bulbous, strawberry-dimpled nose. Then smiled and shook his head.

While we prepared to run before he called 999 and a squad of armed police and dog patrols encircled the pub, he got up and shuffled towards us. As he reached under the counter and pulled out a glass, Bobby and I looked at each other. Had we actually got away with it, or was he going to demand we leave our fingerprints on the glass so he could pass them on to the Authorities? *

Then beer squirted into glasses and Bobby laid three coins on the counter before we joined our co-conspirator at the booth. An old lady sitting across the room looked at us without interest, and Old Bob had retreated to his stool and made no move that we could see to phone the local armed response team. Silently, we lifted our glasses and clinked them together.

'Cheers,' said Mike, 'anyone fancy a fag?' but the effect was spoiled when his voice broke as he casually reached for the group packet of five Woodbines.

~

Elvis Presley's mum bought him a guitar when he was eleven. He beat me by a couple of years, which may be why he was better and more successful than I.

Earlier in the year I'd tried to make a guitar as a first step on the road to rock 'n' roll fame. I used a combination of the plywood and broomstick from the redundant tea chest bass, a bundle of kindling wood borrowed from the shop and a strip of lino.

I added some lengths of catgut from my brother's fishing line and tensioned them round six nails at the top of the broomstick. It looked as unstable as it proved to be when it imploded when I tightened the strings.

My parents were duly sympathetic, and the result was the most exciting Christmas present I can remember.

Although a teenager, I was still a man-child, and went to bed on Christmas Eve with a pillow case pinned to the end of the bed. Although I now knew where the presents came from, I still woke several times in the small hours to find that Santa Dad had not arrived.

The third time I crawled to the end of the bed, the pillow case held only a couple of comic albums, some nuts and an orange. Disappointed, I was about to climb back under the covers when I found a large plastic bag propped against the bed end. It had obviously been too big to fit into the pillow case. As I unzipped and reached inside the bag, there was a twanging sound which set my pulse racing.

I sat on the bed and looked in almost stupefaction at the shiny, sensual curves of the soundbox and the glittering strings and mother-of-pearl dots in between the frets. In my hands I held the key to fame and fortune. I sat back in a stupor of euphoria on that cold and early Christmas morning. All I had to do now was learn to play my new guitar, try and sing in tune, and of course, do some more work on my quiff.

I know I might appear to modern sensibilities to have been overegging the pudding when talking of hearts pounding or escape plans made when we lit up an illegal fag or first went into a pub to try and get served. But in those far-off days, most young people really did respect or even fear the police and other authority figures. The idea of giving a policeman lip or getting up to some really anti-sociable behaviour just did not occur to us. Attitudes have of course changed since the 1950s, and distinctly so by the time the Swinging Sixties came to an end. I will leave the reader to judge whether all those changes were for the good.

1958

~ At 3:04pm on Thursday the sixth of February, a plane crashes shortly after taking off from Munich airport. On board are a young Manchester United side, flying home from a Euro cup tie. Amongst those killed are seven players. Manager Matt Busby is seriously injured

~ Philosopher Bertrand Russell launches the Campaign for Nuclear Disarmament

~ Work begins on the MI, Britain's first full-length motorway

~ Serial husband-killer Mary Wilson is the last woman to be sentenced to death. At the last of her four weddings, she joked that the sandwiches would be fresh enough for her new husband's funeral. He was dead within a year.

~ The Church of England gives its moral backing to Family Planning

~ The last Debutante is formally presented to the Queen at Holyrood

~ The first parking meters are introduced

~ The first clothes boutique is opened in Carnaby Street

~ The first Little Chef opens

~ In Portsmouth, The City Skiffle Contest finals are won by The Checkers, who are awarded the ten pound first prize. An audience of blind people are entertained lavishly by the Portsmouth Players.

Top Tunes

Big Man ~ The Four Preps
Come Prima ~ Marion Marina and his Quartet
Kisses Sweeter than Wine ~ Jimmie Rodgers and (separately) Frankie Vaughan
Kewpie Doll ~ Perry Como and (separately) Frankie Vaughan
Lollipop ~ The Chordettes and (separately) the Mudlarks
Nairobi ~ Tommy Steele and The Steelmen
Great Balls of Fire ~ Jerry Lee Lewis
Peggy Sue ~ Buddy Holly and the Crickets
Jailhouse Rock ~ Elvis Presley
Stupid Cupid ~ Connie Francis
At The Hop ~ Danny and the Juniors
April Love ~ Pat Boone
Good Golly Miss Molly ~ Little Richard
Swingin' Shepherd Blues ~Ted Heath and his Orchestra
When ~ The Kalin Twins
Bird Dog ~ The Everly Brothers
It's Only Make Believe ~ Conway Twitty
Poor Little Fool ~ Ricky Nelson
High Class Baby ~ Cliff Richard
Endless Sleep ~ Marty Wilde

I used to play around with hearts
That hastened at my call
But when I met that little girl
I knew that I would fall
Poor little fool, oh yeah
I was a fool, uh-huh
(Uh-huh, poor little fool)
(I was a fool, oh yeah)

Poor Little Fool performed by Ricky Nelsen. Lyrics by Sharon Sheeley

As teenagers found they had money to spend on fashionable clothing, colour was transforming the sepia tones of everyday life in Portsmouth. Not all were welcome arrivals, and I quote pink iridescent socks as a fair example.

The temples of change were to be found in the coolest clothes shops in Commercial Road, and Shirt King was the brand leader in the Brighter is Better crusade.

Not having the money to indulge in the latest fashions, my little gang had to make the best of what we could afford, scrounge, or sometimes steal.

Having an older brother, I was better-off than Bobby and Mike. John was generous with his cast-offs, especially those which had got torn or bloodstained in what he and his mates and opponents liked to call a 'bundle'. Sometimes he just got fed up with something that he had worn at least twice and found to be 'unlucky'. By this he generally meant it had not worked as a crumpet magnet.

Being taller and wider than me, his cast-off jackets

fitted where they touched, but that was okay as drapes were then all the rage for those bold enough to wear them. I was not looking for trouble, but could at least pretend that my inherited jackets were supposed to be longer than the norm. My favourite was a huge black and white flecked 'salt and pepper' woollen coat with hugely padded shoulders. It was so thick, heavy and well-insulated it could have stood upright without me in it, and was fiercely hot in anything but the coldest situations. Underarm deodorant was still uncommon if not unknown in our circles, and I found a spray bottle of the cheapest and rankest scent I had won at the fun fair did the job. It also made other blokes and girls think I had been successfully on the pull, which was not yet the case.

The fashion then was to have only the bottom button on your jacket done up and the coat worn almost off the shoulder to make you look bigger and hopefully tougher. Together with the padding, my shoulders were so wide I had to turn sideways to get through narrow doors.

Under the coat would be a pink shirt shot through with golden thread and my tie of choice would be a red 'slim jim', as narrow as the coat was wide.

Trousers had to be black and as tight as possible. Almost skin-tight 'drainpipes' were the most *outre* and admired, so the skinnier your legs, the cooler the look.

It seems strange now, but respectable parents kept a thoughtful eye on their sons' trousers and some even measured the bottoms to ensure proper standards of decorum were observed. According to the mores of the day, seventeen-inch-wide bottoms were acceptable; anything less was an assault on good taste and conformity. Some boys would attempt to narrow their trousers by using clothes pegs on the inside, but it was a dangerous business and the result was unconvincing. Mike Beacon was lucky as he had a sister who was good with a needle. She would run a stitch down the inside of each leg before he went out for the evening, and he would unpick it before returning home. When she overdid it, in his big blazer with the badge removed and literally skin-tight trousers and sashaying down the street to meet us, he looked not dissimilar to Professor Max Wallofski (ask your mum or grandmother) doing his funny walk.

Amongst the most desirable of footwear for our age and attitude would be ankle-high canvas 'baseball boots' as favoured by American street gangs, or crepe-soled suede or leather shoes in the winter months. Country music star Carl Perkins even wrote a 'rockabilly' hit song warning about the dangers of standing on his blue suede shoes in 1955, later covered and taken to new heights by Elvis Presley.

I couldn't see myself being able to afford suede shoes before leaving school, but was really proud of a pair of 'apple box' leather shoes, laced up through brass rings, with the crepe soles adding almost two inches to my height. They were my pride and joy, brought back from a Hong Kong street market by my Uncle Bill. He'd got them for next to nothing, he said, as they were at least three sizes too big for the average Oriental male foot. They were actually a bit on the large side for me, but okay as long as I didn't change direction too sharply and leave them pointing straight ahead.

Together with my heavily greased Elvis quiff, barn-door shoulders, pink shirt and yellow socks, I must have looked a real sight patrolling the local manor with my two best mates. I thought my swaying swagger looked menacing and cool, but observers probably thought I was having a problem staying inside my apple boxes.

~

I'm standing at the Priory Crescent bus stop. It's not raining or that cold, but I'm disguising my school uniform beneath my new beige duffle coat. As with jackets, it's almost compulsory to wear it off the shoulders and have only the bottom toggle done up. I don't need to worry about being caught without my school cap on, as it is early evening and I'm not going to the Tech. It's prize-giving night and, having no proper assembly hall, the ceremony is being held at a nearby girls' school. I won't be troubling the prize presenters, but attendance is compulsory, so we bad boys will sprawl sullenly in the back row and glower at the winners and maybe beat them up outside afterwards. I would not be joining in any attacks, but rather acting as a minder and my protection money to be paid in sweets and homework answers.

Then Bobby Harrigan appears from the darkness, long and lean in his black mac with the collar turned up and his small quiff rigidly in place. It is not as impressive as mine, but I know he doesn't put the work in on it. This is because he is nowhere near as vain as me and much better looking, so doesn't need to try too hard. I know my pride and joy is in good shape this evening, as I spent an hour after tea standing sideways-on to the mirror on the wall of my bedroom, looking at myself in profile with the aid of a hand mirror. I spend hours like this every week, checking my nose is not growing too fast, that every hair of my quiff is in place, and how bad my acne-ridden neck looks. I had started pulling my collar up to cover the angry red blobs, but hunching my shoulders made me look slightly deformed.

Bobby arrives at my side, looking white-faced and clearly troubled.

'What's up,' I ask, 'got your bird in trouble?' This was of course not possible, as I knew that he, like Mike and me, was still a virgin and did not even have a girlfriend on hand-holding terms.

'Half the Man U squad have been killed,' he says flatly.

'Oh yeah,' I respond, rubbing my chin to show I know it's a wind-up along the lines of the one about a famously shaven-headed film star. The trick was to say "Did you hear Yul Brynner's dead?" and then add: "Lack of 'air."

But then I realised Bobby was not joking' and it hit me like the news of a relative or close friend dying.

It's hard to describe the significance of that tragedy at Munich airport. It's not easy in such different times to make comparisons, but the shock news had as much if not more impact than the death of Princess Diana. Twenty-three people lost their lives that evening, but the fact that seven of them were young, healthy sporting stars with a great life ahead of them was regarded as a national tragedy.

~

Although bicycles, motor bikes and the odd horse and cart still outnumbered cars, the street scene in the city continued to change apace. As well as the human tragedies and misery it brought, the Portsmouth Blitz had altered the face of our city irrevocably. Some of the changes were to be welcomed, as privately owned slums were replaced with blocks of council-owned and run flats. But, in the process of regeneration, the remains of some grand Victorian dwellings, churches, emporiums and even characterful slums were swept away.

The last and biggest bombsite to be filled-in and built upon was my gang's adventure playground at the junction of Elm Grove and Green Road. Conan Doyle's surgery. My ancestor's first home in the city, the church where I had got my head split open, and the imposing drapery store where HG Wells spent a miserable three years were gone. In their place stood rows of shoe-box-shaped blocks of flats. Much-needed accommodation, but it was sad that there would be no more digging for buried treasure or tobogganing down the slopes of giant craters on the roofs of Anderson shelters.

One reminder of the recent past was still with us, though, National Service remained in force, and it would be two years before the call-up was abolished. Brother John escaped because of his apprenticeship, but his older friends reluctantly went off to paint coal and peel potatoes and learn how to kill people. Nearly everyone agreed it was a good way of instilling discipline in young men, by which I think many older people meant breaking their spirits. A surprising number of victims of the scheme agreed it had been good for them, but only when the memories were summoned from the nostalgic past. Whether it was a good idea or not, National Service was a rite of passage for millions of young men, and almost a mark of honour that you had done your time. I sometimes think I might have enjoyed the experience, but that may have been because I didn't have to.

Other aspects of everyday life in Portsmouth had not changed that much. Trams had long since disappeared, but more than a hundred trolley buses ran on nine routes throughout the city. Thousands of dockyard maties still poured out of the gates at going-home time, though there were fewer of them, and an increasing number of mopeds, motor bikes and even the odd family car would be seen amongst the rampaging horde.

Sailors still came ashore in their 'Seven Seas' horizontally-creased bell-bottoms, but there were fewer to be seen in the pubs and on the streets or laying comatose through drink, violence or both in shop doorways. This was because the Royal Navy was in the throes of post-war decline due to the shrinking Empire and hard economic times. From its peak of 800,000 in WW II, numbers had dropped to 125,000 officers, seamen and Royal Marines 'borne on the books' of the Admiralty.

~

The Milton Skiffle Kings were also of the past, but the Rhythmic Three had taken the stage - or would dearly love to. Given my noted lack of musical talent, Mick Beacon suggested the new name should be The Rhythmic Two Plus One but Bobby

Harrigan and I outvoted him.

Bobby had by now acquired a real snare drum and Mike had found a white jacket to go with his superb singing voice, wispy moustache and quiff. He claimed it was the same type of coat as Marty Wilde wore on stage, but to us it looked more like the sort worn by Verrecchia ice cream van drivers. Mike's quiff was as high and even more pointed than mine, but because of the short-back-and-sides his mum insisted on, it posed no real threat. I was still barred from singing, but had mastered three chords on my guitar. They were G, D and A, which I am told are the most-used chords in rock 'n' roll music. This may be because they are amongst the easiest to play. I tended to make them fit for any song in our repertoire, and in spite of that, Bobby and Mike's close harmony was a delight, particularly when performing Everly Brothers songs. Lacking a proper echo chamber, they had found a way to simulate one, and it could almost be Phil and Don crammed into the outside toilet. As Bobby said, it was a shame we wouldn't be able to take the bog with us on tour when we hit the big time.

~

So, we had a new name and a growing playlist, but had still not staged a proper performance. We were also running out of friends who could be bribed into attending a gig in my bedroom.

Then came the chance of a proper performance in front of a real, live audience. Wimborne Road school youth club was holding a Christmas party, and a friend of Bobby's mother had suggested us as part of the entertainment. On the evening of our debut, we arrived on foot and lugging our gear to find that our name had not been put on the posters, and later found this was because the teacher who created them couldn't spell 'rhythmic'. As we stood and looked on, the stage was occupied by a spotty youth doing bird song impressions. He could only do a cuckoo, crow and owl, so his act did not last long. He was to be followed by a ten-year-old tap dancer who I noted wore plimsolls, and top of the bill was a seedy-looking man in a stained evening suit and no teeth who did things with balloons.

After negotiations with the teacher in charge, we set up in a classroom next to the assembly hall, wedged the door open and belted straight in to 'Wake Up Little Suzie'. Bobby and Mike did a great job on snare drum, castanets and vocals, and my three unamplified chords weren't enough to put them off the melody.

For an hour we went through our whole set, though our audience was confined to our mothers, a teacher with a wonky hearing-aid and a stream of children looking for the toilets next door.

But it was our first proper gig, and gave us a taste for performing in public. There was also a consolation prize for me when I won the Mr Elvis Presley Lookalike Eyes competition. As the lady school teacher confided to my mother some time later, it was my quiff and curled lip (she actually thought it was the result of an operation for a hare lip) that did it. I thought it more likely the fact that the only other entrants were the spotty bird impersonator and the toothless balloon strangler, who also had a severe squint.

~

I don't know if a cure has been found for acne since I had it, or if perhaps there are better ways of disguising it nowadays. For sure I don't seem to see so many sufferers wearing pink pancake make-up or unnaturally hunched shoulders.

Perhaps it was a bad diet or a lower level of personal hygiene, but in my day lots of young people had to walk around with faces like badly-made pizzas. Those with untroubled skin couldn't see what the fuss was about, and those who were afflicted got little sympathy and were the target of all sorts of cruel taunts. Some more insensitive boys obviously didn't care, and the enterprising Dougie Cooper even set up pimple-squeezing tournaments to see who could spatter a mirror from the furthest point.

Although I liked to act tough, I was ultra-sensitive about my appearance and becoming increasingly concerned about the eruptions appearing on my body. My face was fairly clear, but a miniature mountain range of red, angry, pus-filled pimples ran from my neck across my shoulders and down my back. Looking over my shoulder in a mirror it seemed I was wearing a cape of red polka dots.

As they spread, I became obsessed with hiding the damage, and avoided taking my shirt off in company, which meant not going to the baths or beach.

Then I found what I hoped would be a solution. It was very much of its time, though is still around and probably much improved.

In a little white squeezy plastic bottle, Clearasil was,

said the makers, a flesh-coloured ointment which would camouflage the spots while treating them. Actually, it dried into a bright pink poultice which highlighted rather than disguised the problem, but it was all we had.

Another embarrassment was the sprouting of underarm hair, and with it the dramatic increase in perspiration levels. As I have noted, underarm deodorant did not exist, or if it did, we did not know about or have access to it. It got so I would keep my blazer on at all times in school, and would even invent excuses to avoid any activity where I had to take it off. Keeping my blazer on made the stain under my arms worse, and my peculiar stiff-armed and hunched posture was attracting attention from boys and masters.

In the end, a kindly teacher phoned my mother and asked if there was a problem. Perhaps, he asked, she was putting too much starch in my shirts?

~

It was about this time that I joined in a school activity that I really enjoyed. It was putting on a uniform and running around making lots of noise and pretending to kill people.

The Combined Cadet Force had an army and air force contingent, and was under the general command of Colonel 'Sambo' Slade. He was a mostly easy-going physics master, who probably missed the War and was trying to recreate the culture and camaraderie.

I remember him as a short, beefy, red-faced chap who underwent a quite dramatic metamorphosis when in uniform. He would strut around, slapping his swagger stick against his thigh and talking in that curiously reversed services way of putting the object first. It was perhaps the inspiration for Yoda from Star Wars.

When I had put my uniform on for the first time and we met in a corridor, he acknowledged my awkward salute by tapping his officer's hat brim with his stick, then looked me up and down and said: 'Ah. Webbing belt, East for the use of...' before marching away to get it sorted.

To the horror of some parents and masters, we were issued with ancient Lee-Enfield rifles for training exercises. Even in those days, however, we were not routinely given live ammunition. My rifle had a well-worn look and date of manufacture stamped on the stock and I could not help but wonder if it had killed anyone during the First World War.

Our training activities took place at a military establishment at Gosport. For shooting practice at the range, we were issued with live ammo, but for war games it was blank cartridges only. At least, that was the idea, and there were stories of the odd live round being unleashed.

I liked the discipline of shooting, but the most fun was had with the Thunderflashes. These were about the size and shape of a stick of dynamite, and defined in my dictionary as 'a noisy military pyrotechnic device, used in training and which are noisy but not dangerous'. The writer has obviously never been to a Technical School CCF exercise. My favourite position during a mock battle was in a tree, lying in wait for an enemy patrol to pass beneath before igniting and dropping a Thunderflash in their midst. I would aim to miss, but sometimes the 'flash-bang' would get uncomfortably close. To my knowledge, nobody in the CCF was killed or injured badly during my time at the Tech, but it must have been a close thing.

It's sobering to think what great fun it was pretending to maim and kill each other, while for some of the masters it had been the real thing such a relatively short time before.

~

News of a tragedy, and one that made me feel ashamed for myself and my schoolmates.

Chemistry was a favourite lesson; not because it helped us understand the structure and properties and importance of matter, but because it provided so many opportunities to make smells and noises, play pranks, cause minor damage and generally misbehave. The fact that our teacher was so timorous made our behaviour even worse. There were regular minor injuries, mostly caused intentionally. A favourite trick was to play a Bunsen burner on the brass handle of a swan-neck tap, then ask a classmate to turn it on as your hands were full. Blisters were common and first degree burns not unknown.

Our teacher was Mr Jones, a small, slight and un-assuming man with an almost apologetic air. It was naturally a struggle for him to keep control, and at times the atmosphere became completely anarchic.

One morning as the end of term approached, we were in high spirits and particularly unruly. Order had steadily deteriorated, and ten minutes before the bell it broke down completely. Test tubes were thrown, chairs overturned and poor Mr Jones stood in front of the blackboard, pointlessly banging a pointer on his desk and calling for quiet.

Then, the door opened and there was sudden and utter silence.

Framed in the doorway was Gus Gates. To his credit, he did not speak to us or Mr Jones. He just looked around the class with his deadliest death-ray stare before nodding to our teacher and quietly closing the door. It was more than enough to restore order.

Mr Jones took early retirement after the summer break, and the next we heard of him was at morning assembly. In quiet and level tones, Gus Gates said that our old chemistry teacher had passed away on the Isle of Wight.

Later, we heard that he had killed himself, and I wondered how much our behaviour had contributed to his sad end, and how we could have treated him so much better.

~

As well as my close chums and band-mates, I now had an ever-growing number of casual acquaintances. Sometimes they would be customers.

If I went on my bike to school, my self-appointed henchman Little Freddie would ride along. He was clever and genuinely enjoyed lessons, which alone was enough to make him unpopular. I was his informal minder, and he repaid me by trying to get me to understand the mysteries of algebra and why it mattered if the square on the hypotenuse was always equal to the square on the other two sides of any triangle. Or something like that.

On our rides, Freddie would also brief me on the key points of the homework I had not done. If we took the school bus, he would negotiate with the boys who would have the most accurate homework and doctor it for me so it would not look copied. In return he could rely on my protection from bullies. It was a good working relationship as long as I only had to look tough.

Payback time came when Freddie arrived one breaktime to say he was being picked on by a well-known bully. The boy was in the fifth year and an inch or two taller than me, but I reassured myself I had the weight advantage if it came to anything. As I was about to learn, my opponent knew a lot more about street fighting than me.

When I found and asked him if he'd stop trying it on with my little mate, he stood back, looked me up and down, gave a lazy smile and told me to fuck off unless I wanted some as well. I was now in a sticky position. I couldn't swallow and walk away or it would be all over the school and my hard-guy rep destroyed. If I took him on, I could get a nasty beating and lose face in more ways than one. In the end, I accepted his offer and we met for battle in the traditional location behind the toilet block.

I had been knocked down twice and was really getting the worst of it before a prefect was attracted to the noise from the spectators. He quickly broke the fight up and took us to see Gus Gates and his constant companion, the very whippy bamboo cane.

He listened carefully and politely to our claim that it was a friendly fight which got out of hand, then awarded us two strokes each. Afterwards, the prefect told me that it would have normally been a tariff of four strokes apiece, but the omniscient deputy head knew what was behind the fight and had cut the penalty in half for my benefit. He couldn't give me less than the bully, and would for sure find a good reason to give him another helping.

I was left with a black eye and a split lip, and the knowledge of what it was like to be well beaten in a proper fight. On the plus side, my reputation as a defender of the weak and small spread even further and resulted in a queue of small boys holding bags of sweet tributes.

~

Another cast-off from my casually generous brother, and at last I owned a pair of genuine suede shoes. John said he could not bring himself to wear them again as he had spilled vinegar on them in the chip shop after a heavy night out.

It was another reason for me to love and be in awe of my big brother. I not only hero-worshipped him; I wanted to be him.

Though highly intelligent, he had even less interest in learning than me and confused the spelling of ghost and toast till he died. Physically, we were different in several ways. He was over six feet tall at 14, and very handsome. He had a snub nose and wide jaw, tiny ears laid close back against his head, strong white teeth and curly, dark hair. He excelled at sports, had played cricket and soccer for St Luke's school and had a naturally laid-back and affable way with him. That meant he was admired and liked by and always made male friends easily. Also, the combination of his personality, generosity and looks made him a natural wow with the girls.

John was four years older than me, which was quite a gulf in those times. He had been born at the start of the war and so had vague memories of air raids and Anderson shelters. He was a genuine war baby, while I just sneaked in under the ropes. Another gulf because of a few years difference in our ages was that John had left secondary school and started an apprenticeship before I left Cottage Grove. Now he was 18, earning good money and spending his weekends at favoured pubs and dance halls like the Savoy, where he could take his pick of the available talent. His best mates were renowned Pompey hard nuts, and they feared nowhere or nobody.

~

It's a sartorial irony that young men who have to dress smartly for work like to pay a fortune for the sort of clothes we used to wear for dirty manual jobs. In my day, men who got dirty for a living would dress up to the nines for a night out.

It was an early start on the buildings, but that did not stop my brother making the most of his freedom every night…and how I envied him. On a weekday he'd spend an hour or two at the local and at chucking-out time go to someone's house for a game of Three-Card Brag. If in the mood, he and his mates might end up at a late-night haunt like The Milk Bar or Jerry's kiosk on the Hard. Here a young man-about-town could take his choice between chatting up any available girls or having a fight with an available sailor.

With the arrival of the glorious weekend, it was down to the seafront and the Savoy Ballroom and South Parade Pier, sporting one of his collection of suits from Jackson the Tailor of Commercial Road. John was always a stylish dresser and Jackson was a popular choice. For around £14 you could get a made-to-measure suit to your design in just two weeks. At today's prices that would be the best part of £300, but clothes were expected to be expensive and important if you wanted to impress the ladies.

Most members of my brother's set would have several suits made a year. Sometimes when they tired of one, they would simply give it away. I knew of one local hard nut who would often turn up to work on the building sites in a knee-length drape that had been bloodied in a Saturday night set-to.

But that all lay in the future for me. I and my fellow band members were still much more limited in our choice of entertainment, and if not practising our repertoire of hit tunes we would walk for miles around Milton, literally all dressed up but nowhere to go.

Every Friday evening, I would sit on John's bed and watch him prepare for a special end-of-the-working-week night on the tiles. I can see him now, putting on his classy three-piece suit with double vent at the back, button-down-collar shirt and tie and adjusting the matching handkerchief before teasing out his modest quiff and slapping on the Old Spice. Then he would ruffle my hair and be off to the fleshpots, leaving me with his spare change and a burning desire to follow in his footsteps.

When he'd gone, I would pinch a shake or two of his hair tonic and aftershave, then go to my room. There, I would ignore my homework and spend hours gloomily regarding my spots with the double-mirror trick and working with my guitar on discovering, as my dad used to say, the lost chord. Or any more than the basic three I could manage.

~

I don't know if my ever-growing quiff, second-hand suede shoes and stolen dash of Old Spice helped, but I had my first sexual encounter as Christmas approached. Sadly, it was to be an awkward, embarrassing and even humiliating experience.

Quite suddenly, we three best mates had found ourselves girlfriends. Or rather, the band had, and there were only two of them.

Jan and Mary were regular visitors to Wimborne Road Youth club, and after they watched us rehearse and still came back for more, we appointed them President and Secretary of The Rhythmic Three fan club. It was early days and members numbered eight if you counted us, our mums and the girls. Perhaps more surprising than they liking our music was that they were both lookers and could easily have done better than us.

Jan was the oldest by a couple of years and was pretty in a doll-like way. She wore her hair in a pony-tail and was tall, with long, shapely legs and prominent breasts. They were not large, just hiked up under her chin after the fashion of the day. I don't know if the idea was to make the wearer look sexy or provocative, but when pointed at me they looked more than a bit scary.

Mary was shorter with fuller features and her dark hair worn in what I was told was known as a bob cut. She wore her skirts short and tight, and favoured chunky sweaters which did little to disguise her very large breasts. When we had first seen them, there had naturally been some debate on how big and natural they were and what they would look like if set free. Bobby thought she might stuff handkerchiefs or even tea-towels up her jumper and be quite flat chested, but Mike was sure they were all hers. He spoke with the authority of someone who had a sister, and an older one. He was used to seeing stockings and brassieres and panties hanging on the line in the garden or drip-drying over the bath. The other paraphernalia and even the attitudes of femininity were more than familiar, while all Bobby and I knew about the opposite sex was what we heard from other, mostly older boys. Though we lived in matriarchal establishments, they were very male-oriented homes. We knew that the heads of the households were female, but mothers were of course totally different from girls.

~

After a while, the girls became more than our fan club organisers, but there was a problem with the uneven ratio. There were two of them but three of us, and even the concept of *menage a trois* was not within our realm of understanding.

I can't remember whose idea it was or even if it was a formal arrangement, but the problem was solved by taking it in turns to 'go out' with each other.

One week it might be Bobby holding hands with Jan, and Mike alongside Mary as I trailed behind during our evening promenades. The next week it would be my turn to step out with one or other of the girls, and one of the boys would be the odd one out. It was all very innocent, and there were no promises of eternal bonding, or carnal relationships beyond a snog.

Then something happened to change the relationship irrevocably and leave me even more frustrated.

It was a wet Sunday afternoon, and we had been allowed to gather in Mary's mother's terraced house in Fratton. In the middle room, the Dansette record player was plugged into the ceiling light socket, and a standard lamp gave just enough light to see each other. Mrs Sullivan had left us with a plate of sandwiches, a big bottle of cider and instructions to behave ourselves and gone with her latest beau to the pictures.

It was the first time we had been left alone together in the house, and there seemed something special in the air. Officially, it was my turn to be Mary's temporary boyfriend, but it seemed she had more in mind. We'd been sitting on the sofa watching Bobby and Jan gyrating to Elvis's most successful double-sided hit. Mike was DJ for the evening, and when he had put Don't be Cruel on for the fifth time and gone in search of a fish paste sandwich, Mary leaned over and whispered almost conspiratorially in my ear, asking if I would like to see her room. She said she had a photo of James Dean on the wall above her bed, and he looked just like me, except his quiff was better.

For some reason my knees felt weak and she had to help me up and steer me towards the door. In the narrow passageway, she pressed me against the wall as she stood on tiptoe and put her lips against mine. Then, two very unexpected things happened almost simultaneously. The first was when I felt the heavy softness of her breasts against my chest and her silky tongue slipped into my mouth. The second was when I felt the front of my trousers become a tent. My heart beating wildly and my face suddenly hot, I tried to back away, but she giggled and pressed herself even closer.

Somewhere between euphoric anticipation and terror about what might be about to happen, I followed Mary up the stairs like a condemned man ascending the scaffold and not sure how he should feel about what was to come.

Inside, the room smelled enticingly of her. The aroma of perfume and powder was intoxicating, and I remember thinking it would hopefully cover the odour of the sweat running down from beneath my arms.

It was a small room and too dark to see the photo of James Dean, and within two steps I found myself on top of the bed, with her between me and the counterpane.

As the strain increased on the trouser front, I had a momentary picture of the fly buttons exploding, and it got worse as I felt her take and guide my hand to just below where her skirt had ruched up around her fulsome thighs.

I got the message, steeled myself and began my journey of exploration. It was the first time I had had my hand above a girl's knee, let alone beneath her skirt. I knew what was up there, but not exactly where or what form it would take.

The thumping beat of Hound Dog almost kept pace with my heart as she gave a small groan of what I hoped was pleasure and opened her legs a little wider. Then, suddenly I reached the point where her stocking tops gave way to an expanse of uncovered warm flesh.

Her tongue probed ever deeper into my mouth as I tried to breath and steady myself for the next stage. I knew roughly where my hand should be heading, but not the exact location. I'd seen any number of black and white photographs in magazines allegedly extolling the joys and freedoms of naturism, but there was always a strategically placed beach ball or tennis racket covering the vital area. I had of course seen Samantha Stott's front bottom all those years ago at Cottage Grove school, but she was a little girl and Mary was almost a proper, grown-up woman. Had things changed or re-located, and if so, to where?

Another deep breath and I pressed on, and encountered the pantie line. Thinking if it were to be done it were best done quickly, I shoved my fingers beneath the elastic and on through a secret garden of silky hair…and suddenly it happened.

Mary gasped and I froze in utter panic. I had been searching for her most private of places, but had obviously gone off-piste and stuck my finger up her bottom.

I had not known what to expect, but I knew from my own explorations what the inside of my bum felt like.

Aghast at my mistake, I snatched my fingers away and rolled off her and the bed.

She lay in frozen silence until I made a weak and yammering excuse and crawled towards the bedroom door. At least I knew where that should be and what it felt like.

~

Whether or not because of the incident in Mary's bedroom, our *menage a cinq* came to an end when the girls deserted us to become groupies of a local rock 'n' roll band with gigs booked, much more sophisticated instruments and even red tuxedo stage jackets with matching bow ties.

The memory of my first, fumbling engagement also became less of an embarrassment when I realised after further exploration of the female arrangements below the waist that I had not, in fact, put my finger in the wrong place…

1959

~ American pop stars Buddy Holly, Richie Valens and JP 'The Big Bopper' Richardson die in a plane crash with their pilot in Iowa

~ Mowtown records is founded in Detroit by Berry Gordy Jnr

~ The UK grants Independence to Cyprus

~ 20,000 'Ban The Bomb' protestors attend a CND rally in Trafalgar Square

~ British racing champion Mike Hawthorn is killed when his car hits a tree in Guilford

~ An Icelandic gunboat opens fire on British trawlers in what will become known as the Cod Wars

~ The first Juke Box Jury is shown on TV, hosted by David Jacobs

~ UK postcodes are introduced as an experiment

~ BMC introduces a ten-foot, two-door, 848cc four-cylinder car known as The Mini

~ The iconic Bush transistor radio is launched

~ Ian Fleming's Goldfinger is published, and Ivor The Engine makes his first appearance on TV

Top Tunes

It Doesn't Matter Anymore ~ Buddy Holly and The Crickets
Living Doll ~ Cliff Richard and The Drifters
Dream Lover ~ Bobby Darin
Side-Saddle ~ Russ Conway
What Do You Want (If You Don't Want Money) ~ Adam Faith
Running Bear ~ Johnny Preston
Fool Such as I ~ Elvis Presley
Venus ~ Frankie Avalon
He'll Have to Go ~ Jim Reeves
Sweet Nuthin's ~ Brenda Lee
Way Down Yonder in New Orleans ~ Freddie Cannon
Lipstick on Your Collar ~ Connie Francis
Red River Rock ~ Johnny and The Hurricanes
Tiger ~ Fabian
Poison Ivy ~ The Coasters
Never Be Anyone Else But You ~ Ricky Nelson
Here Comes Summer ~ Jerry Keller
Teenager in Love ~ Dion and The Belmonts
Only Sixteen ~ Craig Douglas
Peter Gunn ~ Ray Anthony and his Orchestra
What D'You Wanna Make Those Eyes At Me For? ~ Emile Ford and the Checkmates

Dream lover, where are you
With a love, oh, so true
And the hand that I can hold
To feel you near as I grow old
'Cos I want (yeah-yeah, yeah)
A girl (yeah-yeah, yeah)
To call (yeah-yeah, yeah)
My own (yeah-yeah, yeah)
I want a dream lover
So I don't have to dream alone

Dream Lover performed and written by Bobby Darin

A new decade lay in wait, and I could see light at the end of the educational tunnel.

At my age, my dad and most of his generation would have already started work to help support the family. In the generation before theirs, fourteen-year-olds would have been regarded as adults and able to sign up and go to sea. Those previous generations had had little choice, but I was still at school and wanted not to be.

I was still reading comics and playing silly street games, but dreaming of doing man's work, going up the pub, getting a motorbike and doing it with a real girl and not just my hand.

Physically, I was losing some of what my mother called puppy fat, but had stopped growing upwards and felt cheated. This was because my dad was born in the slums of a city renowned for its stunted men, yet had reached a height of nearly six feet five inches. My brother had made it to six feet one, but I got no further than five feet ten. Above average for those days, but I had regarded it as my birth right to be at least as tall as my brother. This may be why I began to feel threatened by anyone taller than me, and why I would fight with them at the least excuse. I guess a psychologist might say it was because of my feeling of resentment at my lack of inches, but my Glaswegian granny said it was just because, like my dad, I liked a 'square go' (fight).

Although I had stopped growing upwards, other indicators of approaching manhood were appearing. There was hair growing ever more lushly under my arms and round my lower belly, but frustratingly not on my face. In spite of shaving twice a day (it was claimed that would make the bristles appear and grow more quickly) my cheeks remained, as my dad used to say, as smooth as a baby's arse. Although Mike Beacon had his downy blonde moustache, we all yearned for sideboards. Not enormous, bushy creations like Elvis, but respectably full and just to the bottom of the ear lobes. Don't ask me why, but any lower on the jaw was seen as a challenge in the rule book of ritual male confrontation. For a while we would draw and fill side-whiskers in with Mick's sister's eyebrow pencil before going out. From a distance or at a glance in a bad light they looked quite realistic. The problem came when we were out and it started to rain and our carefully styled sideboards would turn into small brown rivulets and give the game away.

~

It may not have been a popular view, but I rather liked school dinners. Mind you, I've always enjoyed hospital food. But I was never a fussy eater and I suspect today's school dinner customers or hospital patients would sue for unnatural cruelty causing long-term mental effects.

I'd been no more than an onlooker at Cottage Grove as the giant vacuum tureens arrived by van, and had felt oddly resentful that I would not get to share what was inside. Now, home was three miles away, so I became a dinner boy.

There were two sittings, and as you approached the shabby hall it was obvious which prefect and master was on crowd control. If they were disciplinarians, there would be an orderly line; if it was a pair of softies, mayhem would ensue. Any excuse would do for a scuffle, but there was actually a good reason for fighting to get to the front of the queue. As there were two sittings, those winning a place in the first would get the least overheated food and bigger helpings.

To be fed, you needed a ticket, and a booklet for the week was five bob (25 pence) or around £5 at today's prices. Boys from poor families got free tickets, but they were a different colour and let everyone know whose mum and dad couldn't afford the price of a hot meal for their son. Some entrepreneurs amongst the older boys tried to forge tickets, but the price of discovery was a visit to Gus Gates and far too painful to be worth the risk.

Once inside the single-storey brick and asbestos hall, boys made for one of the eight-seater tables, and cronies and classmates stuck together. There would be a head of table, and he would often pick his dining companions with as much care as if selecting a soccer team. One notorious and gigantic Jabba-the-Hutt lookalike crewed his table with small boys so he could have the lion's share. I suppose another option if he was still hungry after the meal would have been to eat one of them.

When places had been taken, the duty master would inspect each table and select the order in which each would go up to the serving hatch. The toughest invigilators were reckoned to be Bill 'Captain' Blood and 'Sambo' Slade, and it was not unknown for a slovenly or unruly boy to be sent out without his dinner. Sitting up straight with arms folded and a non-insolent look on your face would help win your table priority

There was no menu, and the choice was take-it-or-leave it although there was the vegetarian option. This was an enlightened attitude for the times, but those who did not eat meat were usually regarded as a bit suspect. Usually, the vegetarian alternative would be to leave the meat off the plate or, in season, choose a salad or a hard-boiled-egg dressed with some grated cheese and carrot. Actually, as the lettuce leaves were often skimpily washed and slugs missed, the salad was not always strictly vegetarian.

A typical offering for the rest of us would be some form of alleged meat and two veg. Steak pie was a weekly regular, with the gristly meat lurking beneath pastry squares served with mashed potato as lumpy as a bag of marbles and gravy which was even lumpier. Then there would be carrots and watery cabbage, boiled to within an inch of their lives and the greens mashed as skimpily as the potatoes with the edge of a saucer. For some reason the cabbage had a pungent odour that outdid the most malignant odours from the chemistry lab, sports changing room or even a superfart from the school champion, Jumbo Fatty Atkins.

Another favourite of whoever planned the meals was beef stew, served with the signature lumpy mash and the meat so tough and gristly that some boys would still be chewing on it when afternoon lessons started.

In summertime there would be the same sort of salad as the vegetarian choice, sometimes garnished with a see-through wafer of corned beef.

Puddings were often disguised with custard, sometimes coloured pink or white and strangely and even suspiciously unlumpy. Regular arrivals would include Flies on An Island (a raft of pastry with currants on top floating in a sea of thin custard) or Frog Spawn (tapioca pudding) and Wall Paper Paste (semolina pudding). My favourite was steamed suet pudding with currants and custard. Known to most as Spotted Dick, but to our table as Syphilis Pudding.

In these days of multi-choices and healthy-eating initiatives and allergy or intolerance warnings at most school canteens, it's hard to believe most plates were cleared and boys actually looked forward to dinner time. But in those harder times, many would have found - even if they would not say so - school dinners to be better and more plentiful than they were used to at home.

~

Along with my outsize salt-and-pepper jacket, plum waistcoat, gold thread button-down collar shirt, vinegar-stained suede shoes and day-glo luminescent socks, I was now also tooled up and apparently ready for bloody battle.

Along with imitation pearl buttons, the waistcoat had two front pockets. I suppose they were originally designed to hold a pocket watch or train ticket; In mine I kept a top-up tube of Clearasil for acne emergencies and a condom. It would mean I was ready for action in the unlikely event of getting lucky, but was really there to impress my mates. In those days, condoms came in surprisingly (to me) large brown paper envelopes, which may have been why the common name for them was French Letters.

Poking out from each pocket would be the tops of a pair of ivory-handled cutthroat razors. They belonged to my uncle Bill, who stayed with us when home from the sea. He now used a patent safety razor, and I had borrowed them from his 'ditty box', the small wooden chest in which sailors traditionally kept needle and thread and personal items and souvenirs.

Before going out, I'd stand in front of the mirror and practise whipping both razors out and flicking them open in the face of an imaginary adversary. Of course, they were there just for show, and I would never have used them. It was just a young boy trying to look tough to himself and his mates.

Unlike today, in those times weapons were commonly for show and rarely used. Some Teddy Boys liked to wear large sovereign or knuckleduster-type rings or carry sharpened bicycle chains. The theory was that apart from lashing out with them, the chain could be wrapped round the fist to add weight to a punch. I doubt this ever happened in a real punch-up, as it would make much more of a mess of the user's hand than the recipient's face. A traditional and purely defensive precaution was to have fish hooks or razor blades sewn into the back of your lapels. The idea was that anyone trying to get a grip before nutting you would get a nasty surprise. I don't know how popular the idea was, but knew one wannabe Ted who forgot he had got his girl to sew a range of hooks in place. He grabbed both lapels before sashaying down the street in the approved manner and hooked himself to his coat.

I don't know if it's the same today, but a simple walk along most streets in Portsmouth in those times was a testing time for young males. How you walked, what you wore and how you wore it and even the expression on your face declared your readiness to prove how hard you were. In a coffee bar or dance hall or anywhere there were young females, it was even more so. If you wanted safe passage, it was best to dress quietly, keep your eyes to the floor and walk circumspectly. And definitely not to ask a local hard-nut's bird if she fancied a dance.

In any public location, you had to be careful who you looked at and for how long. 'Who you screwin' moosh?' was a standard challenge, and was an invitation to take things further or back down and hurry past with bowed head.

Amongst Teddy Boys, even the length of your jacket could be a statement of willingness to get involved in a dust-up. The hem of a jacket reaching to the knuckles of a clenched fist held by your side was a fairly safe option and showed you were not generally up for bother. A fingertip-length drape indicated you fancied your chances, and anything below that was the equivalent of a gunfighter in the Old West wearing his six-gun on show and strapped menacingly low.

I knew some boys who carried flick knives, and a few years later I carried a little .22 pistol. It looked more like a cigarette lighter than a gun, and, like the razors, was just for show. I would never have used it, and in any case I had no bullets for it. It was just a conversation piece, or to flash if the odds seemed a bit high. I think the big difference with today is that, where we made a big deal out of looking and acting tough and sometimes carried weapons for effect, young men who go about tooled-up nowadays seem prepared to use them, and sometimes to deadly effect.

~

We wannabe Teds had our local heroes, and Hughie Finnegan was a legendary style guru. He was also the best-looking and well kitted-out Ted I ever saw. He had a lush quiff and sideboards which looked long enough to knot under his chin. He was almost impossibly handsome and, though short of stature, a man not to cross. In later years I was to join his younger brother's gang, but at this time I was in quivering awe of him. I recall standing behind Hughie in the queue for a film at the Troxy cinema in Fratton Road. He was wearing a drape which reached to his knees and a pair of perfectly cylindrical drainpipe trousers. He was holding hands with his girl, and as we shuffled forward he looked casually over his shoulder. In the future he and his brothers were to become good friends, but as his eyes rested on mine that chilly evening, I felt my bowels turn to water.

"Who are you lookin' at, mush?"
Hughie Finnegan (far left) and local Teds

~

Another use for one of my few talents.

As if wanting to upmarket and improve its image ready for the new buildings which would replace the wooden huts and tired classrooms, the Technical High School was to field a rugby XV.

The Technical High School's first rugby team. My rebellious nature shows with the dirty shirt, worn on the outside.

Though I was not sporty, I was big and burly, and was soon approached by the two masters behind the scheme. A small and twinkly man with a moustache and a pin striped suit, Mr Heke said I had come to his attention because of my reputation for not backing down from a confrontation, which would be a valuable asset. My complete lack of knowledge of or interest in the sport was immaterial as it would be a new activity to all of us. Boys making up the team, he added casually, would get special privileges. When I asked what they would be, he said they might include time off from lessons for training, free kit and what he called 'sympathetic' judgement of my class work. Another incentive was the orange slices at half time.

As I reached for the pen, he observed that as well as the right temperament, I had short legs, a long body and was severely overweight, an ideal combination for a useful hooker.

~

As well as having an empty bookings diary, The Rhythmic Three was lacking a place to practise for the gigs we didn't have.

We'd outstayed our welcome at Wimborne Road Youth Club after members of the weekly Hard of Hearing group had complained. Mother had also received a deputation about the row from my bedroom from neighbours, and there was even talk of some customers boycotting the shop after being exposed to my version of Guitar Boogie Shuffle.

I was hurt as I was making an effort and had invested in top British guitarist Bert Weedon's Play in a Day manual. Even after a month it had not worked, and my range was still limited to the three basic chords. The trick was to pick songs for our playlist into which they could be fitted.

Then, Bobby arrived with news that he had found us a new rehearsal room.

He had met a nice if plain girl, who had obviously taken a shine to him. She was not much to look at, but the good news was that her mother was profoundly deaf and would be happy for us to practise in her front room. Also, her mum did not get on with her neighbours so quite liked the idea of us disturbing their peace.

From then on, we spent at least three evenings a week at Madge's house, practising our leg movements, head shakes and lip curls as well as existing and new tunes. It was not a time of originality, and like all amateur groups we just copied the hits of the British artists who copied the American artists who had the big chart hits. Ironically, many of the USA 'original' hits were copied from earlier, little known records from little-known artists.

Along with the new practice room, it was exciting to find we were building a new fan base. Mostly, they were a handful of younger girls who would sit on the forecourt wall or play hopscotch while we laboured away on Shakin' All Over or Be-Bop-a-Lula. But there was also a handful of Madge's schoolmates who would be admitted to the front room to watch us rehearse. Two of the girls were so-so, but one a real stunner.

Jilly was a year or so older than the rest of us, and already at work. That gave her extra status amongst her still school-bound friends, and meant she could afford to buy the latest fashions and have her hair done professionally. In those days, most parents couldn't afford to lash out on fashionable clothes and shoes for their children, which was another reason why so many of us were so keen to leave school and get a job.

Jilly was my height in her fire-engine-red high heels,

and dressed to make the most of what we used to call an hour-glass figure. This was a term coined to describe female film stars with big tits and bum and narrow waist. It might seem sexist nowadays, but I never heard a qualifier complain about being awarded the compliment.

From the top of her head to those high heels, it seemed to our adolescent minds that every aspect of Jilly's appearance was calculated to drive us mad with lust. Her gleaming, tawny hair swung seductively as she moved her head, and was cut in the 'page boy' style later made ultra-fashionable by designer Mary Quant and Eurovision songstress Sandy Shaw.

To emphasise her voluptuous figure, Jilly liked to wear a closely-fitting white blouse secured by eight small black buttons (I undid them constantly in my head and bed) with a high, frilled collar and a cameo brooch neckband. The blouse accentuated her fulsome breasts. The narrowness of her waist was emphasised by a shiny, tight, six-inch-wide plastic belt.

Below that, our pulsating libidos were driven into a frenzy by what was known as a pencil skirt. Worn to great effect by Marilyn Monroe, Jane Russell and other Hollywood stars with wide hips and narrow waists, it reached an inch or two below the knees, its shrink-wrap effect relieved only by a small vent at the back. It was usually worn so tight it made walking difficult, and the consequent hobble was considered very sexy. With Jilly's, you could even see the ridge of the top of her sheer black stockings and the bump of the suspender belt buttons. Her way of flopping down on the sofa then easing the skirt over her hips would make me play even more bum notes than usual, and the boys to break their usually impeccable harmony. The sexiest sound imaginable was the rustle and squeak as she crossed or uncrossed her long legs or ran a blood-red painted fingernail along her thigh, and the artful performance would literally put our drummer off his stroke.

In contrast to all this perfect pulchritude, Jilly had a lazy eye. In a man it would have been called a squint and a source of derision; in Jilly Gould, the slightly off-focus gaze seemed wildly sexy.

She was my fantasy lover for several months, and I lived in hope that I would get the chance to rectify my humiliating under-skirt fumblings of the previous year.

Sadly, it never happened. Talking about it years later, Mike and I discovered we'd both imagined that Jilly was sending meaningful signals to us alone as she wriggled on the sofa and cast her suggestive looks our way. In fact, it was the tall, cool and laid-back Bobby she went off with, and I suppose the confusion may have been because of her misdirected but so, so seductive lazy eye.

~

No practice for our band on one dark February evening, as we and millions of pop fans around the world are in mourning. The previous year, the loss of eight of Manchester United rising stars had stunned a nation. Now, the world of rock and roll music had lost three of its best-known stars.

At just 17, Ritchie Valens already had two hits

under his belt, and *La Bamba* was to become an all-time classic. Musician, songwriter and disc jockey JP 'Big Bopper' Richardson had a huge and immediate chart success with the novelty song Chantilly Lace. Then there was Buddy Holly. Born to a Texan musical family in the Great Depression, Holly had begun his career as a warm-up act for Bill Hayley and Elvis Presley. Then came *That'll be the Day* and Peggy Sue, both his compositions and both chart-toppers.

The three stars were on a tour of the mid-west, and Holly chartered a plane to take them from Iowa to the next gig in Minnesota. The plane crashed shortly after take-off, and we will never know how many more great songs Holly would have written and performed. Such was the reaction to the tragedy, it became known as The Day the Music Died.

~

At school I was counting down to Freedom Day, and bullying bullies who were smaller than me, enjoying the cadet force and rugby sessions almost made those final months bearable.

In the CCF I got to run around, pose heroically and pretend to shoot people; in rugby I got to hog the ball, run around and knock people over.

My knowledge of the rules of Association Rugby was sketchy to the extreme. I knew that the general idea was to win possession of the ball, then get it over the line for a try, then kick it over the posts for a conversion. It's not that I have forgotten the finer points of the rules, just that I never learned or was much interested in them.

As I learned, the hooker's main job was to be nasty to the opposition players in the scrum. He also tries to win the ball when it's thrown in to the melee by 'hooking' it towards a member of his team. Another important function comes when the ball has gone out of play, and the hooker throws it to where the two teams are lined up. I was quite good at throwing, and especially of making a nuisance of myself in the scrum. Otherwise, when the ball came my way I would just put my head down and go for the line. Because of my direct and very unsubtle approach, I became known as The Tank by my fellow team members. Members of the other side who got in the way had other names for me. I, who was so frustrated at having no talent for any sport or musical activity, was bemused at how simple it was to do well and win praise from my peers and masters.

During our first season I won honourable mentions in the school magazine, had a try-out for Hampshire Colts and was finally poached by Havant, a top local team. This was seen as an act of treachery by my team-mates and the teacher who had persuaded me to start playing the game. I liked being wanted, but after a couple of meetings with him and other staff members, a mix of threats and bribery persuaded me to return to the school side.

As one of the teachers said, as long as I didn't become too familiar with the rules, I could have a future in the sport.

I considered the prospect of lots of training, doing what I was told and having my Friday nights out curtailed, and decided I would not be a happy hooker. Later and after leaving school I would take my aggression out on the streets rather than playing fields.

Life is what it is, but I sometimes wonder how different mine would have been had I been wearing my thinking head when, not for the first time, opportunity knocked and I did not hear it.

~

As what should have been my learning years drew to a close, Mother announced that we were moving on. After four years of long hours and putting up with customers, she had decided it was time to make a change. She had sold Kay's Stores and would work from home on her various entrepreneurial activities, while Dad would become the main breadwinner. Or that was the plan.

She told me that she had bought him a snooker hall which was almost a going concern. It was down-at-heel, had a bad reputation and lurked behind a greengrocery in London Road. The eight tables had more stitches in them than Frankenstein's monster, and the catering facilities consisted of an old pot-bellied stove to heat up the tea pot and meat pies that had not escaped. That, said Mother, was why she got it so cheaply; but with a bit of hard work and attention she was sure it could become a successful business. And, she said finally with a familiar glint in her eye, if my father made a hash of it, she would take over and make him and it pay.

Big night out. After hours of primping and preening, I'm ready for my visit to the local youth club.

Our new home was no more than a mile distant from Kay's Stores.

An unassuming three-bedroom, single bay-and-forecourt in a pleasant area of Milton. No. 6, Cromarty Avenue lay behind St James's church, tucked away from the main road and just a stroll from Milton Park.

After the boarding house in Castle Road and then the shop, it seemed strange to live in a place where nobody was going to turf me out of my room or where I would meet complete strangers in the toilet. Neither would there be a constantly clanging bell as customers arrived in the front room or tapped urgently on the window outside of hours. I had lost the status of living in a sweet shop, but as I got older that had less appeal to my mates and any potential girlfriends.

A further cause for optimism was that I'd heard there was a girl living in the locality who was a real goer. The wasteland around nearby Langstone Harbour was known locally as the humps 'n' bumps. Although an unattractive terrain of rubble and concrete, it was a popular place to visit for people with rubbish to dump or no good to get up to. It was especially popular as a venue for courting couples. Humps 'n' bumps Hilda was said to be a particularly frequent visitor with different escorts or sometimes even two at the same time. With any luck, this could be my big chance to use my willy for its, at this time of my life, most important purpose.

~

A big evening.

With school over for the week and the glorious weekend laying ahead, it was to be my first visit to the youth club at Eastney Modern School.

Young people complain nowadays that there's nowhere for them to go or nothing to do outside the home. This is of course a load of codswallop, especially as they nearly all want to spend endless hours locked in their rooms with their phones and tablets and PCs trying to kill a competitor's avatar in the next road or half way round the world. In those days there really was nothing much for adolescent and early teens to do, and the youth club was a brilliant place to meet your mates, pose around and stare lecherously at members of the opposite sex.

Because it was my first visit, I would be taking special care with my appearance, and had spread the various potions and implements on the bed like a surgeon laying out his instruments.

First would be a close shave I did not really need, using my dad's patent Rolls Safety Razor. This was a curious device which was sharpened by pushing it up and down a decorative metal box. Then a leisurely bath, heavily laced with Mother's aromatic bath salts. The chunky pieces were said to soften the water and make you smell good, but took a time to dissolve and left an imprint on your bottom if you got into the tub too quickly.

Now came the most important part of the procedure: Operation Quiff. The washing and drying and fixing my hair in place took at least an hour, and the aim was to get every hair in place and to my complete satisfaction, then set it as rigid and damage-proof as the prow of an icebreaker. It might seem a lot of fuss and somewhat effeminate, but I know for a fact that some of the hardest blokes in Pompey spent more time on their hair than many girls.

There were no conditioners in those days, and the most popular shampoos had seductive names like Sunsilk and Supersoft. I was going easy on washing my hair after an overdose of a preparation advertised as The Hilton Shade Lighter Look. At this time Billy Fury had the girls swooning with his blonde quiff, so I wanted to lighten up my mousy-toned locks. According to the instructions, you worked the mixture into your scalp in small amounts over the course of some weeks to make your hair a shade or two lighter. I was impatient, so used the whole bottle in one session and my hair had turned almost white overnight. As it was my first visit to Eastney Youth Club, I hoped it would be assumed I was a natural blond or even a part-albino.

After the wash, it was on with the Amami Wave Set lotion. Along with advertisements voiced by football pools tipster Horace Batchelor, Amami featured frequently on Radio Luxembourg. This was the only commercial radio station in our universe, and so rare we actually enjoyed listening to the ads. Like countless other young people, I would strain to hear the ebbing and flowing strains of the latest pop tunes in bed every night, and some of those oft-repeated commercials must be engraved in a million memories.

The trick with the Wave Set was to apply the gunk liberally, then set it like quick-drying concrete by the application of heat. Unknown to my friends and hopefully the males in my family, I had an oversized hair net which I would ease over the freshly-combed quiff to keep it in shape as I blasted it with Mother's ancient hairdryer. I would know when it was sufficiently set when smoke rose from my head and the smell of singed hair filled the room. When the hairnet was removed, the quiff would withstand the strongest wind, and even do a good deal of damage if used to give someone a Glasgow Header.

As well as the hair dye, I was avoiding the use of my sun lamp. It looked like an oversized light bulb set in a metal frame, and I'd got it on prescription from the NHS for use on the growing welter of spots on my back, shoulders and neck.

Aware of my growing embarrassment, Mother had taken me to see the bemused doctor, who had shrugged his shoulders and referred me to St Mary's hospital. There, I attended a number of sessions in a ward next to the VD clinic. The treatment started with the nurse scrubbing my back with an ointment filled with grains of sand. This was to remove the top layer of skin and free the pores of the blackheads and release the natural oil I was over-producing. That didn't work, so the next experimental treatment was to pierce each spot with a cocktail stick, then squeeze a drop of acid into the mini-crater. The idea was to literally burn the pustule away, which the acid did, but left my back looking like the surface of the moon.

Finally, the doctor in charge had prescribed me the sun lamp, which, he hoped, would dry out the grease clogging my pores and causing the spots. I had taken to using it on my face in the hope of achieving an interesting tan. In fact, it turned my face beetroot red, with panda-like white rings where the goggles fitted.

Now the crimson tide was receding, and I would dab on the Clearasil to try and disguise any pimples that had crept up above the collar line. The problem was that the pink lotion would transfer to the shirt collar, but if anyone noticed I would pretend it came from a girl's face on my shoulder rather than a tube of anti-pimple cream.

~

At last and after no more than a couple of hours, I was ready for my first visit to my new local youth club.

Mother took a snap of me on the doorstep, and I have it still. My nervous half-smile seems to show a mix of apprehension and anticipation and is as stiff as my towering quiff. I'm wearing an Italian-style box-jacketed suit inherited from brother John, a white shirt and 'slim jim' red tie, relatively sober socks and my allegedly calfskin moccasins. Chewing steadily on my Dentyne teeth-whitening gum, and after checking with a cupped hand for the tenth time that my breath was sweet, I posed for the camera, touched my quiff yet again to check it was in place, and set out to find a girl whose single admiring look would make all the effort worthwhile.

~

In my parents' time, plain girls who were rarely invited onto the dance floor were called wallflowers. The pretty ones would be under constant assault from would-be partners. At youth clubs in my day, this was very much not the case. I don't know why, but the general rule was that the girls danced with each other, and we blokes watched. There was always something to see and wonder at.

We were still in the process of emerging from drab, post-war Britain, but female fashions and hairstyles were evolving at a pace. More sophisticated girls (or those who wanted to appear sophisticated) might wear what was called a French pleat. If pulled back and secured too tightly, it gave the wearer a permanently surprised look. Nowadays I believe it can be known as an Essex face lift.

Then there was the glorious bouffant, which actually dated back to the 17th century and was re-popularised by the likes of American President's wife, Jackie Kennedy. The word came from the French for 'puff up' and that was certainly the case.

An even more extreme example of creative back-combing was the 'beehive', which piled the hair up by as much as a foot with the help of sugar water and even bits of cardboard to support the weight. A flock of female pop stars would make the style popular, but to me they made the wearer look like she had just got off the back of a motor bike and forgotten to remove her helmet.

From girlfriends prepared to reveal their boudoir secrets, I would hear tales of rags, giant curlers and wincingly hot leaf-blower-type domestic hair dryers attached to the head with plastic bags. Then there was the increasing use by 'bottle blondes' of the acrid chemical hydrogen peroxide. The fashion began with film goddess Jean Harlow, who used a lethal combination of peroxide, household bleach and ammonia to get the look she wanted. It was all the rage, but had such a bad effect on her hair that she ended up wearing a wig. Next came natural brunette Marilyn Monroe, who was said to bar other blondes from any film set she worked on. Another dangerous DIY trick at this time involved fashion victims putting their heads on an ironing board so their hair could be straightened by a hopefully steady-handed friend.

As to feminine clothing, 'pedal-pushers' or matador trousers and even jeans had yet to become widespread amongst working class girls on our side of the Atlantic, and how you dressed would depend on your finances or access to an older sister's wardrobe. The youngest girls would wear cardigans over school shirts and skirts, while the older ones would mostly be wearing dresses or skirts of varying volume. Some were loose 'swing' skirts, while others were known as 'crinolines' because they were puffed out by layers of fluffy petticoats.

Then at the other end of the scale were the really tight skirts, known as hobble or pencil or even wiggle skirts. They suited girls with natural knock-knees, and some wearers could only jive or bop by hopping and turning in tight circles. This meant they normally took the male role when dancing with a friend. The more daring girls in full skirts and dresses would delight in spinning and causing the hems to rise to reveal a flash of stocking top and white thigh. At a time when it was rare to see a female knee in normal circumstance, this could be a truly arousing sight.

~

I spent most of my first visit with my back to the hall wall in bouncer stance, hands over my crotch and trying not to make eye contact with any but the softest-looking males. I was also painfully aware of being weighed up by the girls. With most it would be an apparently casual glance; with the bolder ones it would be a stare of cool appraisal, which made my lamp-burned face glow even redder.

Now and then I would turn my head so a dancer I fancied would get what I believed to be my best profile. This was the start of what became an obsessive habit, where I would move my head slowly and deliberately to show my best side and not disturb my quiff. It became so pronounced that new girlfriends would often ask if I was suffering from a stiff neck.

In youth clubs held in schools, the main action would always take place in the assembly hall. At Eastney, the music came from a fairly modern record player on a table on the stage. Connected to a series of loudspeakers, by day it was used for music appreciation lessons; by evening and with the volume cranked up to the top level the supervisor would permit, it would blast out the latest hits.

After an hour of rating the dancers for face and figure, wondering which one might be humps 'n' bumps Hilda and whether I would ever have the nerve to ask for a dance, I checked it was not raining or too windy for the integrity of my quiff and went outside.

In the playground, a football was being kicked about by some sporty-looking youths, and I saw that a fellow rugby team member was teaching a small youth how to disable an imaginary machete-wielding attacker.

At first sight, Butch Mason appeared as wide as he was tall, and he was not short. Had he been available for the *Goldfinger* James Bond movie a few years later, he would have been a shoo-in for the part of Oddjob. He had a vast frame, huge arms, legs and hands and a head that looked as if it had been borrowed from the Easter Islands. It would be fair to say that he looked more than menacing, and even as if he ate rats for breakfast. Actually, he was an inoffensive and obliging young man. He taught unarmed combat at the club, and if anyone had no need of weapons it was Butch.

Over by the gate I saw a huddle of bikers, kitted out with studded leather jackets, oily jeans and knee-high boots. Recognising one as a customer at Kay's Stores, I walked over and found the centre of attention was a tall, gangly young man, sitting astride a very small motorcycle. It was so small his knees seemed to reach almost to his chin. I recognised it as a Francis-Barnett 125, a two-stroke with a high-pitched sound and a subject of derision for bikers well-off enough to afford more powerful bikes. In those days, two-stroke engines were considered girly; proper bikers had the rumble and roar of a four-stroke at their command.

I realised why the little knot were so admiring of the Fanny-Barnet when the bell rang to signal the club was closing and they made for the bike shed, mounted their bicycles and pedalled off. One was even wearing a crash helmet. Although they had the gear, none were old enough or could afford to buy any sort of motorcycle. Like me, they longed for a real motorbike with which to impress the girls and even carry one off on.

My chance to own an absolute legend of the motorcycling world was to come much sooner that I had thought. In fact, it came too soon.

~

The Indian Chief was fire-engine red, with the profile of a native America hand-painted on the tank. It must have been built around twenty years before I was born, and of the type seen with siren blaring and being ridden by cops in pursuit of the bad guys in old gangster movies. It had hugely wide and high handlebars, a gear stick on the tank, a tractor-style seat and footrest boards that hinged upwards when the rider leaned it over to take a sharp corner.

Altogether it was wondrous, and up for sale. The asking price was a bit over thirty quid, but it would have been beyond my means at a fiver.

A friend of a friend had told me about the Indian, and when I saw it, I knew I would die if I could not have it. I wanted it even more than Hank B. Marvin's Fender Stratocaster, or sex with Jayne Mansfield. Well, perhaps not more than having sex with Jane Mansfield or even humps 'n' bumps Hilda, but certainly more than a Fender Stratocaster (see later).

After sitting astride, firing it up and feeling the throb between my legs and the booming echo of the exhaust bouncing off the garage walls, I went straight home and begged my mother for a loan. I would, I promised, pay her back in instalments as soon as I got a job in the coming year.

Although usually indulgent to my whims and wishes, Mother stood firm. As she pointed out, I was too young to ride it, it was obviously a death-trap and would cost a fortune to make roadworthy. Finally, how did I think she would feel if I killed myself on a machine that she had paid for?

She was, of course, right, but I still think of what it would have been like to own that beautiful monster. Especially when I read recently that a similar model, once owned by a movie star, had sold at auction in New York for the equivalent of £250,000.

~

Although on a much more modest machine, I had my first motorised ride shortly after seeing the Indian Chief. It convinced me that I was born to be a biker.

A slightly dodgy mate of a schoolmate had acquired an ancient moped (he didn't say and I didn't ask from where) and invited me to try it out. If I liked it I could have it for a fiver and pay in instalments. He would even keep it in his garage so my mother would never know.

Dusk fell as I sat astride the rusty machine in a lane behind Fratton Park. The vendor pushed behind and I began to pedal. Nothing happened and I increased the frenzy of my pedalling, then suddenly the engine caught. I still remember the exact moment when the motor took over and pulled me along, my feet doing no more than resting on the pedals. I doubt I was travelling at more than fifteen miles an hour, but with the wind in my face and the owner left far behind, I thought I was flying.

I gave him a pound when I returned, pushing the bike as it had run out of petrol. He was as good as his word, and kept the bike for me in the lock-up garage. It was only when I returned for my next ride that I learned neither the bike nor the garage was his, and he had sold the old French *Mobylette* to five other would-be easy riders.

~

Midnight had come and gone and I was sitting on the edge of my bed, looking into the mirror on the wall. To my surprise, I didn't look much different. In fact, I didn't really feel that much different, in spite of what had happened. An hour before, I had actually achieved what I had been dreaming of and rehearsing for since my lesson in wanking at the swimming baths.

At last I had done it, and with a real girl.

It had started as just another ordinary evening out. Mike and I were at a loose end as there was no band practice. Bobby was on a date with Madge Butler (part of the informal charge for using her mum's front room for our rehearsals), and we had decided to see what was on at the flicks.

Arriving at the Essoldo and feeling past the age of bunking in, we had paid our one and ninepences and managed to install ourselves directly behind two girls in the row in front. For those not having the nerve or wit to try and chat up females face to face, this was common practice in darkened cinemas across the land. Boys would position themselves behind any promising talent, and spend the evening making what they thought were witty comments about the film, slipping in asides about themselves and their adventures, and maybe even the girls in front and their hairstyles and scent. This ploy allowed us to talk casually about the motorbikes we didn't own, the pints we claimed to have downed and the punch-ups we hadn't actually been involved in. Not much fun for people sitting nearby, but of course we didn't think of them.

An hour later and we had got no reaction to our amusing badinage. Then the lights came up for the intermission and one of the girls turned round and regarded us coolly and even calculatingly. After all these years, I remember her face and expression exactly. She was probably a couple of years older than us and wore her red hair down to her shoulders. She had sharp but not unattractive features and I noticed how the school-girlish butterfly clip above one ear contrasted sharply with the heaviness of her make-up. Using our standard parameters would have given her six out of ten for looks, but our relative positions prevented me from giving her a tits, bum and legs rating. As I tried for an Elvis leer, she looked from me to Mike in a curiously impersonal way, then turned back and said something to her friend.

The lights went down, and I sat back to compose some more witticisms when I felt Mike's elbow in my ribs. I turned to see him pointing at the back of the head of the girl who had been weighing us up.

His mouth was working silently and when I frowned and shook my head, he leaned over and whispered in dramatic tones.

'It's her.'

'Her who?' I asked.

'Her,' he said. 'You know...humps and bumps Hilda.'

~

'I'm not doing it down here.'

An hour before, we had followed the two girls out of the Essoldo and along Albert Road. We had trailed behind them, continuing our smooth patter and making subtle complimentary remarks but still being totally ignored.

Then they stopped, lit up cigarettes and after a few words went off in different directions. As she left, Hilda - if it were actually her - looked at me and gave a small nod, indicating that I should join her. It was all very businesslike. Mike and I parted, and though not actually shaking hands, looked at each other like two adventurers going off on a perilous adventure into the unknown. I looked back as business-like I obediently fell into step with Hilda, and saw that the other girl had turned a corner. Mike had clearly lost his nerve and walked straight on.

~

At her direction we stopped at a chip shop, then I followed her into a large park. Unusually, the gates were unlocked and open, and the path led towards Locksway Road, the houseboat village...and the humps and bumps.

My fishcake and chips lay still wrapped on the grass beneath the big elm tree by the far gate. The chip shop had a good reputation, but I was too excited and nervous to eat. Hilda then put the last piece of pink-skinned sausage into her mouth, and stood up.

I followed her and we stood face-to-face as she leaned back and hiked her skirt up with practised ease. I gulped, considered my options, and reached for my zip with trembling fingers.

It was literally all over in a matter of seconds, and I think she must have got far more satisfaction from her saveloy than my clumsy and so brief performance.

Afterwards, she pulled her knickers up briskly and told me there was no need to walk her home. I stammered out my thanks and asked if we could meet again, but she just shrugged, ran her hands through her hair and disappeared into the night. I called a croaky 'good night' after her and I fancy she gave a small smile and a nod of her head as if to signify she knew it had been my first time.

It was the last time I saw her, and I often wish we could have met in later life. If still with us, she would more than probably not remember our brief encounter. But for me it was the start of something really, really big.

1960

- ~ Manchester FC sign 20-year-old Dennis Law for a record transfer fee of £55,000
- ~ Jodrell Bank Observatory makes contact with American space probe Pioneer 5 over a record-breaking distance of 407,000 miles
- ~ Princess Margaret marries society photographer Anthony Armstrong-Jones in the first televised royal wedding
- ~ The Beatles make their first appearance under their new name at a night club in Germany
- ~ The first traffic wardens take to the streets of London
- ~ ITV broadcasts the first live football league match. It will be the last for 23 years
- ~ The Queen launches the first nuclear-powered submarine at Barrow-in-Furness
- ~ 60,000 protesters attend an anti-nuclear weapons rally in London
- ~ The first episode of Coronation Street is broadcast
- ~ Lady Chatterley's Lover sells 200,000 copies in one day on its publication after being banned since 1928
- ~ First minted in the 13th century, the farthing ceases to be legal tender

~ The last 18-year-olds are called up for National Service as Conscription ends
~ American Rock 'n' roll star Eddie Cochran, 21, is killed in a car crash in Wiltshire

Top Tunes

Cathy's Clown ~ The Everly Brothers
Apache ~ The Shadows
Please Don't Tease ~ Cliff Richard
Why ~ Anthony Newley
As Long As He Needs Me ~ Shirley Bassey
Only the Lonely ~ Roy Orbison
It's Now or Never ~ Elvis Presley
Mess of Blues ~ Elvis Presley
Handy Man ~ Jimmy Jones
Good Timin' ~ Jimmy Jones
Poor Me ~ Adam Faith
Tell Laura I love Her ~ Ricky Valence
Three Steps to Heaven ~ Eddie Cochran
Shakin' All Over ~ Johnny Kidd and the Pirates
Theme from A Summer Place ~ Percy Faith and his
Orchestra

When you move in right up close to me
That's when I get the shakes all over me
Quivers down my back bone
I've got the shakes down the kneebone. Yeah!
The tremors in the thighbone
Shakin' all over

Shakin' All Over by Johnny Kidd and the Pirates.
Lyrics by Johnny Kidd

'**A**re you *really* sure about this, East?'

Mr Vine was the careers master, and a kindly man who obviously took his job seriously. So seriously that his face seemed permanently set in an expression of rueful resignation after years of seeing so many pupils casually throwing away the chance of a rewarding career and future. The idea of brighter boys leaving school early seemed particularly painful to him.

In those days it was common practice for fourth form boys to take what were called 'mock' GCE examinations. These would be the papers from the year before, and the idea was to see how you performed in an examination setting. If you got a pass mark in your chosen subjects, the school would sponsor your sitting for the real thing for the next year. if you failed, you could still take the exams but your parents would have to pay the entry fee.

Considering how little attention I paid to lessons, I was surprisingly good at any sort of tests. As one cynical teacher put it, I was a natural bluffer and good at pretending to know what I didn't. Based on my success with the previous year's mocks, I had been sponsored by the school for six 'O' levels.

When I told Mr Vine I wanted to leave school at Easter and would miss the GCEs, he looked even more painfully resigned than usual. When I told him I was leaving so I could help pay my way at home, his shoulders actually slumped. It was an excuse he had probably heard a thousand times before, and he knew it would usually be a lie. He would see my copping out as another loss and failure. As he had learned, sensible boys thought about the future and the need to carve out a career. Others like me just wanted to escape as soon as legally possible. What he knew and we did not appreciate was that having a dirty, laborious and non-challenging job with not much future would not be so much fun in later years.

~

After the long days at school or work, the weekend was special, and had to be made the most of.

For many teenagers, tradition and inclination called for a Saturday morning visit to Commercial Road shopping centre. It gave girls the excuse to dress up and go on show while pretending to be there to meet friends and window-shop. The boys made no secret they were there to look hard or cool and watch the girls go by - and maybe even pull a date for that evening. The first stop on the circuit for most would be the cafeteria at the Landport Drapery Bazaar.

Compared with the posh stores in the Southsea

shopping area, the LDB was a slightly downmarket but go-ahead department store, with such modern wonders as an escalator and a photo-booth in the entranceway. What made it special on Saturday mornings for us was that you could be entertained by Portsmouth's top band while drinking frothy coffee in see-through Pyrex cups.

After winning a heat in the Carrol Levis 'Search for a Star' contest at the King's Theatre, Mike Glover and his Rock 'n' Rollers played in venues across Portsmouth and were the first local group to appear at the Savoy Ballroom. It was Mick Glover and his group that helped inspire me to aspire to rock and roll fame. The success of the band also spawned an avalanche of local pop groups. A few years on, and it would be unusual to walk down any Portsmouth street and not hear the highly amplified twanging tones of an ill-played guitar from at least one front room.

After the session, some would visit Weston Harts next door and listen to the latest records in the booths; others would window shop. If not visiting Shirt King to consider the latest fashions, most of us lads would head straight for Woollies.

The popularity of Woolworth's cafeteria on a Saturday lunchtime was not because of the high standards of its cuisine, but because it was a perfect location for talent-spotting. In an echo of the cinema routine, we would sit near to a tableful of girls or lean over the railings to make what we thought were clever remarks to any talent passing by below. In spite of or because of that, many girls put Woollies on their weekly walk-through agenda. It was a very suitable location to see and be seen, and maybe fix up a date for that evening. Although I never had much luck, I had a mate who did.

Tall and annoyingly handsome, Charlie 'Wacker' Turner had a quiff to rival mine, and bluer eyes than Paul Newman. He also had a laid-back charm and easy manner that appealed to girls and his admirers at our school.

At a time when pulling a bird for a date at a casual encounter was more than rare, Wacker was a local legend. He was never without a pretty girl on his arm for the weekend, and I once asked him, apart from his good looks and wit and charm, what did he think was the secret of his success. He said the trick was obvious if you thought about it. It was to ask every attractive girl he saw for a date. He would fix a different time that evening with those who said yes, putting the most attractive first. If she turned up, he had his date. If not, he would move on to the next one. Nowadays it may seem a thoughtless and selfish act, but getting stood up was a common occurrence and the subject of a thousand sad songs.

~

Unlike Wacker Turner, I was still starved of female company, though I had become a bit of a temporary hero.

My chance to play Burt Lancaster taking on Ernest Borgnine in From Here to Eternity came at the Immanuel youth club in Bradford Junction. At the time, I was kneeling to gather up a dozen cigarettes I'd unwittingly scattered on the floor.

People not of our generation might find themselves bemused by tales of the rituals and posturing young men undertook to impress the opposite sex. Or maybe we just did the same sort of things differently in the foreign country that is the past.

Then, there was a particular way of walking and talking and acting when standing on street corners and watching the girls go by. First, there was the whipping out of your comb to run through your quiff, then turning your collar up, narrowing your eyes and hunching your shoulders. We thought the procedure cool, but to others it must have looked as if we were suffering a mild epileptic fit.

My specialities included rolling or flipping a half-crown between and across the fingers of one hand like movie star George Raft in any of his gangster roles. Another was the way to casually offer a girl a stylish American cigarette from a soft packet. The idea was to hold the pack out and casually flick the bottom. If it behaved as in the movies, one of the cigarettes would obediently rise from the pack for her to take and have lit with my imitation Zippo lighter. Marlboro cigarettes were 'toasted' and tasted awful and very expensive, but as I only used them as a prop, a packet could last for weeks.

It was a tricky operation, and I practised it for hours at a time in my bedroom. On this occasion it went badly wrong when I tapped the packet too hard and sprayed the contents over the floor.

As I gathered them, I heard a scream and saw a group of girls scatter from near the main door. The cause was one of the regular visitors, obviously drunk or high or both. This was not unusual, but then I saw he was carrying a Stanley knife and pointing at a clearly terrified youth. The aggressor was named Bill, and I knew he was a carpet fitter so the Stanley knife was probably a tool of his trade. Sober, he was a rough and ready but friendly type, but had a liking for a mixture of rough cider and aspirins. The youth backing away from him and towards me was Wally, a regular attendee at the church as well as the youth club. He was an office worker with soft white hands and a good dancer, so popular with some of the girls.

I left the cigarettes on the floor and stood up, my heart beating so heavily I thought the girl beside me would hear it. I wasn't feeling heroic, but had seen the chance for a bit of dramatic display in front of an audience.

I had by now grown out of carrying my uncle's cut-throat razors in my waistcoat pockets, and would not have used them anyway. Looking round and thinking about all the bar room brawl scenes I'd seen in movies recently, I grabbed a chair from the side of the hall and walked slowly towards Bill, holding the legs out like a lion tamer. Thankfully, he looked at me, then at the knife almost as if seeing it for the first time, turned and ran out of the hall.

I put the chair back, trying not to show how much my hands were shaking, and bent down to pick up the remaining Marlboros as if the dramatic incident had been no more than a distraction.

I didn't actually get a round of applause or any embraces or even admiring words from the girls, but I felt my status had increased. Another outcome was that my first teenage near-bundle had given me a taste for theatrical gestures in punch-ups.

~

News came that another American rock 'n' roll hero had left the stage. It seemed particularly sad and unfair that Eddie Cochran should come all the way to England to die in a car crash in Wiltshire. He was at the end of a tour, and his latest hit was called *Three Steps to Heaven*.

The song was one of Bobby and Mike's harmony specials, but would be sung by them no more. Not because of the death of Eddie Cochran, but because Mike Beacon was no longer one of the Rhythmic Three. Impatient at our lack of progress, he had joined a local band which was much better known than ours. They had a stage uniform of white tuxedos and bow ties, a drummer with a full kit, and guitarists with proper electric guitars and amplifiers. They even had a sign-written van to carry their gear around in. So we were now to be the Rhythmic Two, or given my tin ear and total lack of ability to progress beyond the three-chord trick, perhaps we should be honest and rebrand our band as The Rhythmic One.

~

The Easter holidays were approaching, and with them my leaving day. It seemed I had been waiting for ever for this moment, but now it was near, it seemed almost too close. Then one morning I heard there could be a job for me to walk into.

Mr Vine called me into his office to say a local branch of a national heating and ventilating company might be willing to take me on. The manager had seen the results of my mock exams and had spoken to Mr Sparshatt, the Technical Drawing master. Mr Vine had made an appointment for an interview with the manager, and if all went well I would be offered a job as a Trainee Draughtsman. This, he said brightly, would mean I would be involved in designing heating and ventilating systems for schools, hospitals and other large establishments. It would be a safe, respected and rewarding career, working in a clean and comfortable office.

I think he knew what was coming, but his face still dropped as I told him I actually wanted to get my hands dirty and earn enough money from the start to buy a motorbike and some new clothes. As well as contributing to the family income, of course. What I didn't say was, that working in an office was regarded as a pouffy job in my circle, while joining big pipes together with a welder's mask on was seen as tough and cool.

The poor man sighed, shook his head and said he would ask about an apprenticeship with the company, then watched sadly as I threw away the opportunity he had created. As it would transpire, I was to make a habit of making the wrong choice and spitting in the face of good fortune.

~

When I told my parents about my intention to leave school at Easter and go to work on a building site, Mother was obviously deeply unhappy. She had always thought or hoped that I would use my brains to pass exams, win certificates and get a good job with prospects.

As she said, she had had no choice but to go and work in a factory when her grandfather committed suicide and the family fortunes collapsed. She would not stop me doing what I wanted, but she couldn't see why I would want to follow in my brother's footsteps. Yes he was earning good money and fine with the physicality of his job, but would he feel the same when he was over fifty and lugging heavy, pipes about a building site? It was, she said, not too late to call the manager at Brightside and tell him I had changed my mind.

When she turned to him for support, my dad merely shrugged and said he had left school at fourteen and it hadn't done him much harm. At this my mother snorted and said it had not done him a lot of good, either.

Curiously and in spite of what he had said, I could tell my father was as disappointed as Mother. He was bright, clever and one of the wisest men I ever knew, but just not able or willing to use those gifts. He knew how the world worked and what people were like, and I think he secretly resented not being able to go to university. In later years he was angered by the way young people were able to go to university to take degrees in useless subjects like managing golf courses. I think, like Mother he would have liked me to be the first East to go to uni. In fact, in later years I did. But, unfortunately, not for long when they found out my entry qualifications were forged.

~

The Rhythmic Three are no more, but a new group has risen from the ashes.

After losing Mike Beacon to an up-and-coming band, Bobby and I spent time finding and recruiting members for our new group. We spent even longer discussing the vital issue of a new name.

There were no rules, except that what we called ourselves should be memorable and cool. Not having an everyday name was the first step on the road to stardom, as so many solo acts had proved. That was why Thomas Hicks had become Tommy Steele, and Ronald Wycherley's management figured he would sell a lot more records as Billy Fury. Reginald Leonard Smith preferred to be known to his fans as Marty Wilde, while Bernard William Jewry would find fame as Shane Fenton, and then reinvent himself with great success as Alvin Stardust. We can never know if they would have done just as well with their real names, but the change seemed to work for Gerry Dorsey when he shot to fame as Englebert Humperdinck after years in the doldrums.

We wanted our new band to sound pacy and cool and something to do with cars. A local group had already taken the cool name The Cadillacs, and we didn't think The Morris Minors or Ford Prefects would have quite the same ring.

After weeks of debate and argument, we agreed on a style of car rather than a make, and so The Dynamic Hot Rods took to the stage. Or would do when we had persuaded someone to give us our first gig.

~

Our first rehearsal was, like the curate's egg, good in parts.

The new line-up relieved Bobby of his drumming duties and free to concentrate on singing. Another advantage was that Johnny Witt had a full set of classy Premier drums. I didn't like to ask him to audition as he was a big, hard-looking guy with a really long drape and an even more aggressive quiff than me.

The Hot Rods would also feature a proper lead guitarist. His name was Colin Quaintance and he had only been playing for a month. I had started him off by showing him my three-cord repertoire, and he'd already left me far behind. That was fortunate, as the main reason I chose someone with no previous skills was that he had an elder brother who was willing to stand guarantor so Colin could buy the most lusted-after non-acoustic guitar in history.

Played by Buddy Holly and Hank B Marvin of the Shadows, the Fender Stratocaster was designed in 1952 but proved ageless, and then it looked like it had been transported back from the distant future. Technically, the Strat was a double-cutaway solid, with three built-in pick-up microphones and a tremolo handle that meant the player can really get a twang going. More importantly, it was as cool as could be.

The new line-up also boasted a bass guitarist. He didn't yet own a bass guitar, but had assured me he would use only the lowest four of his standard six-string model until he could afford a proper one.

Colin Wilkinson certainly looked the part; there was something of the Ricky Nelson about him, and he has worked really hard on his guitar swing and hip swivelling. The trick was to end up in knock-kneed pose with guitar held high, and was considered very sexy in pop group circles. It set the girls screaming when a big rock star did it, though to me the pose looked similar to a polio victim with his leg braces off.

When I first heard about Colin W, I was most impressed to learn that he owned a pair of white-topped shoes, just like the late Eddie Cochran and other big names on the rock scene. It wasn't till I saw him in action that I realised they were his old school shoes with the instep painted white. They looked fine, but, he said, but he was banned from wearing them in the house. This was because his special knock-kneed and twist trick made the Blanco whitening crack and crumble, and his mother barred them because of the mess they made on the front room carpet.

~

My last birthday as a schoolboy, and I marked the occasion by going on a scrumpy run with some new mates from Eastney Youth Club.

I was the oldest in our party but, just as at the Milton Arms, nobody bothered to challenge us.

Nowadays, many pubs ask for proof of age when youngsters arrive; in our day publicans were not much bothered unless they didn't want young people as customers. As long as you had the price of a pint and behaved yourself, you would generally be welcome.

Traditionally, there was much less concern about the standards of behaviour in pubs selling scrumpy. I remember standing in the bar of a city centre boozer and watching a sailor peeing against the bar as he drained a glass of rough cider. The yellow trail ran down the bar front and across the bare boards, and nobody in the pub seemed to notice or care. In notorious dives like The Albany, where Pompey Lil or one of her colleagues might be obliging a customer with a hand shandy under the table, or Peter the Pouffe performing his famed Bottle Dance, someone making room for another pint and not bothering to visit the toilet would have been no big deal.

In those days, every Naval port had its dodgy pubs where scrumpy and blood flowed, and fights were almost as common as a game of darts in a respectable house. Police and licensing authorities allowed these dens of iniquity to stay open as it kept the bad apples out of good pubs. It also allowed the cops to find the bad boys when they wanted to feel a collar. Another bonus was that if the arrest rate was down, they could be sure to find a handful of candidates in any of the more notorious scrumpy houses.

Nobody knows where the name came from, but scrumpy was originally brewed in west county farmhouses to keep the workers going, and was up to three times as strong as standard draught beers. It certainly looked as dodgy as it tasted. While a pint of bitter would be held up to the light to check on its clarity, a good pint of scrumpy was opaque, with bits of apple and other more unsavoury items suspended in the murky liquid. It was rumoured that dead cats or bits of other animals would be thrown into the brewing vat to speed the fermenting process and add a certain piquancy to the flavour. I don't know if this was true, but it certainly tasted like it might be.

Only the less fussy pubs sold scrumpy, as apart

from the type of customer it attracted, it also had a detrimental effect on all the other draught beers served on the premises. It was said that once a glass had held scrumpy it was useless for any other drink. As I learned in later years as a drayman, the leaky wooden barrels also attracted swarms of fruit flies to the cellar. What it did to the insides of long-time scrumpy drinkers could be judged by how years of dripping from barrels would eat away at wooden and even concrete floors.

Known colloquially as Devil's Brew, Head Banger or Sick Horse's Piss, scrumpy was a staple for matelots on a run ashore, those with a big thirst and small pockets, and anyone who wanted to get drunk very quickly. As well as twice the strength of other draught drinks it was half the price at sixpence (2.5 new pence) a pint. Better still it only took two pints to get merry, three pints to get stroppy, and four pints to get into a fight. Another advantage was that you didn't feel any pain when someone thumped you.

I will never know how many pints I got through on my birthday run, or if I had been in a fight with one of my mates, a stranger, or the pavement. It was the first of many blackouts I was to have, and my memories ended when we rolled into the third pub.

I woke with a bloody nose and black eye, and short of a pair of trousers, with a large lady regarding me from her doorstep. I found out later that my mates had carried me home and left me in what they thought was my forecourt before ringing the bell and making off. To be fair, they had got the number of my house right, just the name of the street wrong.

~

A mix of sadness, trepidation and elation as I walked through the school gates for the last time, wearing a black eye but no cap. For the first time since I had learned the rules the hard way, I kept it in my pocket and my tie untightened. I was prepared for a show-down with the Devil's representative on Earth, but Gus Gates merely watched as I walked past. I even detected a shadow of a smile on his skull-like features, and he nodded as if to show he knew what the day was and why I had made my petty point.

~

I'd like to be able to claim the day was spent being wished well by teachers and schoolmates and perhaps even carried out of the school gates shoulder high and seen on my way, but it was not like that.

To the staff and pupils, it was just another day, though I knew I would be missed by the masters in charge of the rugby XV as well as the tribute-payers who had relied on my protection.

I had brought my guitar to mark the occasion, and George Langton had brought his trumpet and bow tie. We took to the stage in the dining hall when the dinner ladies had cleared away, and performed an instrumental version of A Whole Lotta Woman. A big hit of a couple of years earlier, it summed up an era with its twangy guitar and piano riffs, and was written by rockabilly artist and part-Cherokee, Marvin Rainwater.

I remember we had a fair audience of diners, a couple of the dinner ladies and a suspicious janitor,

On my way: my last day at The Tech. Note the slim-jim tie in defiance of the school ruling.

and George performed perfectly on his trumpet. My big moment was when he stopped for me to do the distinctive guitar riff. Holding my breath, I actually hit all the right notes in the right order and even managed to work in a Colin Wilkinson swivel hip pose. But I had forgotten the riff was repeated, and when George stopped and looked at me for the second time, I looked back at him. Then I froze and fumbled and played all the wrong notes in the wrong order.

I remember the incident particularly as it seemed to sum up my life from then on. A promising start but cocked up by over-confidence and lack of attention.

The end of my first week of work, and I had already begun to think Mr Vine may have been right. Leaving school early might not have been such a shrewd move.

I was now a fully indentured apprentice and locked in to the trade for five years. I had assumed I would be learning how to weld and screw pipes together from the start, but all I had done so far was make the tea, run errands to the shop, empty piss buckets and daub lots of red paint on piping and myself. This turned out not to be a good idea, as after its use was banned in the nineties, red lead was to become known as the 'new asbestos'. Mind you, over the coming years I was also to be over-exposed to tons of that deadly stuff.

The Portsmouth branch of the Brightside Heating and Ventilating Company was an undistinguished office and yard on a small industrial estate sandwiched between St Mary's Hospital and Portsmouth FC's home ground.

On my first day I arrived on time and met the storekeeper, a gloomy-looking man who gave me a broom and said I should look busy when anyone appeared. He was tall and stooped and had unusually large feet if his somehow Dickensian-looking boots were anything to go by. His ears matched his feet for being outsize and looked like two back rashers of albino bacon. I noted there was a huge blackhead on the top of one of them. Overall, he was a very pale hue as if he emerged rarely into the light. When I asked if he knew where I would be working, he laughed hollowly and said that was anyone's guess. There were sites all over the south, but if they forgot me, I might be doomed to hang around the stores for a long, long time. One new apprentice, he said with some relish, had spent his first year sweeping up in the yard until someone in authority asked who he was and what he was doing.

Over a cup of tea, Bill explained all the problems he had with his job and that his real interest was as a Samaritan. Listening to his sepulchral tones and general air of gloom, I couldn't help wondering if he was naturally suited to persuading suicidal callers that life was worth living.

It was a relief when, after a couple of hours, the area manager turned up to take me to my first place of work. He was a big, bluff, red-faced man in a tweedy jacket and baggy flannels, with a peak cap, spectacles and an Errol Flynn moustache. We rattled off in his little van to my first place of work, and on route he asked me about my background and how many girls I had shagged. When I had told him about school and lied about the girls, he looked sideways at me and asked why I had been so dense as to sign up as a pipe-strangler when I could have done so much better for myself.

~

I wake with a start to find I've been dribbling and am sitting alone at the back of a bus as it pulls into the depot at Cosham. It's nearly seven and more than twelve hours since I set out from home this morning. I'm the only passenger on the lower deck, and this may be because my overalls stink of me, red lead paint and the sticky putty-like stuff used when joining pipes together.

I had left home in the dark that morning, and walked to the Guildhall kitted out in my new denim work jacket and bib and brace overall. My sandwiches were in an old gas mask bag slung over one shoulder, and my new steel toe-capped boots did not suit walking. My final destination was no more than a dozen or so miles from home as the crow is said to fly, but required three changes of bus and a mile walk down a lane. There was no travelling time or expenses, and my starting weekly wage was three pounds ten shillings. Half of this I would be giving Mother to help with my keep, a pound would be saved for my motor bike, and the rest I would fritter away on drink and, hopefully, wild and willing women.

It did not take me long to work out that I should have given more thought to how much I would be earning, and how much I would be able to save. As it turned out, the answer was nothing, and I soon got into the habit of paying for my housekeeping straight from my wage packet each Thursday, and borrowing it all back on the Monday.

When I did get round to getting some cash together, the bike I wanted was one of a job lot of former World War II dispatch rider's Matchless 350cc, regularly advertised in the Exchange & Market magazine. It would be a bumpy ride as that model had rigid back forks and the only suspension is the big springs under the tractor-style seat. They were all khaki in colour, but I could repaint mine - perhaps with some red lead smuggled off the building site. The price was a bargain at £19, but if I didn't start putting money away soon my apprentice-ship would be over before I could afford one.

~

The building site lay at the bottom of a lane leading from the Hampshire village of Warsash, and was to become a School of Navigation for Merchant Navy Officers. I arrived to find the apprentice from who I was taking over waiting at the gate. He was older than me and astride a shiny new 500cc BSA Shooting Star, which made my mouth water. Ray was a pleasant, open-faced young man, and said he'd hung on so he could mark my card. To start with, he reassured me that the fitters and their mates were not the sort to make me go through the traditional initiation ceremony. When I asked what that entailed, he said that the tradition was for the new boy to be stripped, hung from the scaffolding and have his todger and bollocks covered in the mixture of putty and oil they used to seal screwed-together piping. He also didn't think it would happen because the foreman wouldn't have it. Not because of the humiliation, but the waste of company time and materials. The gaffer was, he added, a right miserable bastard without a sense of humour and had never been known to crack a smile. I was to find Ray was right in all respects. The gaffer was not a bad man, but a stickler for the rules and obviously took his job very seriously. He was what they called 'old school' and one of the millions of workers of minor rank who helped make Britain great by their slavish devotion to duty and doing the job right for no other reason than that it should be.

My martinet boss was a tall, cadaverous man of middle years, with thinning hair plastered back in a widow's peak over a narrow head, a pale face, pointy nose and thin but surprisingly red lips. Unsurprisingly, he was known on the site as Count Dracula. More often than not, I found the men pronounced 'Count' wrongly.

I found him on his back in a muddy trench inspecting a welded joint in a large pipe. When I introduced myself, he stood up, checked his watch, told me I was late, looked me up and down and grunted in a somehow disappointed way. He then led the way to the store shed, where among the sacks of fittings, gas cylinders, masks, goggles, bundles of welding rod and machines for bending or cutting through pipe stood a fifty-gallon drum. It was full, the foreman said, of red lead, which was put on to keep the outside pipes from rusting. My job was to paint every inch of them, and it went without saying I mustn't waste any as it was very expensive. As he spoke, he whipped a compact mirror from the breast pocket of his overalls and flicked it open to show the mirror inside. It was, he said, so he could check I'd painted behind the pipes and not just the visible bits. Then he snapped the compact shut, handed me a four-inch brush and a two-gallon bucket, pointed at the drum of paint and told me to get to it.

I did, and by the dinner break whistle I had got through three buckets of the thick red paint, not all of it on the pipes.

I found my new workmates gathered in the Nissen hut which doubled as a canteen, wet weather refuge and medical centre in the case of accidents. I don't remember ever seeing a first aid box, but there were plenty of trestle tables on which to lay any injured parties. As I was to learn, Health and Safety were just two separate words to most building site workers. Safety helmets and glasses were unknown, and plimsolls or even sandals more common than steel toe-capped boots. Workers worked in high places with no scaffolding barriers between them and a long drop. Despite all this, serious accidents seemed rare. Perhaps as with batsmen's helmets, the lack of protection made workers more careful.

My new colleagues were gathered in one corner, opening packets of sandwiches and unscrewing the tops of vacuum flasks. Some had welding masks or goggles pushed to the top of their heads, and I couldn't help but notice they had not taken their overalls off or washed their hands. Apart from sweat and burned and singed material, the overwhelming reek was of the putty and oil mixture Ray had told me of. It was an odour that would stay with me for the next five years.

One of the younger men was looking dubiously at a plate on which a fried egg and two rashers of streaky bacon were sitting in a layer of congealed grease. He seemed a cheerful type, with lots of teeth, a sprinkling of freckles and a big, bright ginger quiff. He also had sideboards to rival Hughie Finnegan's. He said his name was Charlie and that he was a fitter's mate. That, he explained, did not mean he liked pipe stranglers, but worked for them. He was looking dubiously at the plate because he had forgotten his sarnies and ordered a dinner from Old Bert. He nodded to where a figure was shuffling away from a pot-bellied stove alongside a long table on which were lined up dozens of plates of egg and bacon. They all looked as immoveable on their plates as Charlie's. Old Bert was bent almost double and moving so slowly that I reckoned the food on the plates he held in his shaking hands would be even more mummified by the time they reached their destination.

Charlie explained that the old man had been gassed and wounded in World War I, and his welcome back to a land fit for heroes had been no work. He finally got a job in a tin mine in Cornwall, and was badly injured in a mining accident. There had been no compensation and his pension was pathetic, so at over eighty he spent every morning running errands and making dinners to order. It was a long way to the nearest shop and Bert's bike was nearly as old as him. The menu was the same every day, and he had to start cooking on the stove top a couple of hours before the dinner break. This meant the food would be cold, and stuck to the plate with grease by the time it reached the table. To demonstrate, he turned his upside down. Nothing stirred, and he put it back on the table and pushed it away. I offered him one of my peanut butter sandwiches, and he gratefully accepted. So as not to hurt Old Bert's feelings, he said, he would take the calcified egg and bacon home. If the dog wouldn't eat it, the grease would do nicely for easing the sticky suspension on his motor bike.

~

By five 'o'clock I had gone through another three bucketsful of red lead, and must have got a substantial percentage of it on my clothes and face and in my hair. My hands were also coated, and the paint mingled with the blood running from my grazed knuckles.

The problem was getting at the backs of the pipes, which were held in place only an inch away from the breeze block walls of the trenches and ducts. It was even harder to get at them with a four-inch brush. Knowing that the foreman would be inspecting my work with his compact mirror, I had loaded the brush heavily and sloshed the red lead in the gap between pipe and wall

When he arrived with his compact to hand, the foreman was not too concerned about my wounds, but very unhappy that I had wasted so much red lead. Not just by smearing it on myself and the blocks, but by painting the wrong pipes. The larger ones were, as he had shown me, the heating pipes; the thinner ones running alongside them in the ducts were conduits holding electrical wiring.

When he had silently mourned the waste of company materials, he told me I was finished for the day. The law stated that, as an apprentice I could only work a thirty-eight-hour week. That meant knocking off an hour before the men and coming in for half a day on Saturdays. I had the choice of walking the mile to the clock tower at Warsash and catching the bus, or waiting in the fittings hut for the men to knock off at six. He would give me a lift to Portsmouth in his car, or I could go with my new friend Charlie on his motorbike.

Over the coming months I would vary my routine, either taking the sequence of buses, or waiting for the men to knock off and getting a lift. Either option would get me back to Portsmouth about the same time. So, my working day was about thirteen hours.

It was while I was sitting in the hut and looking at the wall that I wondered why the foreman had not just let me work the extra hour during the week, which would have meant I wouldn't have had to come in on Saturdays.

I asked him about this before I was sent to another site, and he just shrugged, looked at me as if I was being unreasonable, and said that was how it was.

~

Saturday afternoon and the start of my precious weekend.

After the three-hour journey there and back to work just half a day, I would lie in the bath, looking at my toes and thinking how I could pack the most into the break. In a way, having to work on Saturday morning made the rest of the weekend so much more valuable. The hours of soaking in the bath and scrubbing the dirt of a week's work off also made it feel so much better to climb into my Saturday gear.

Because of the morning shift there was no more Mick Glover at the LDB, but with money in my pocket I would head straight for the open-air market at Charlotte Street and The Shirt King. When I was in funds, I would treat myself to a snazzy shirt or a pair of Lee Cooper jeans. I would have preferred Wranglers but they were too expensive. Levis were also out of the question. The Lee Coopers would be almost half a week's wages, but Mother would let me off my rent for that week, which I would have borrowed back anyway.

Because of my short legs, I'd need my mother to cut them to length, leaving plenty for turnups. At that time, cowboy style turnups on jeans was the rule, and even the height of them was important. Finnicky blokes with office or shop jobs and clean fingernails wore jeans with no more than an inch of turnup, and usually above shiny plain brown leather shoes. Some broke the prime rule and cast doubt on their masculinity by actually putting creases in their jeans as if they were suit trousers. Bikers or lairy blokes wore them low on the hip and with a turnup of as much as six inches, hitched up over suede ankle or leather biker boots

My regular shopping spree set back my saving schedule for a motorbike, but I had become a fashion victim. I'd left school and taken on a dirty and demanding job just to get a bike, but there was still not a penny in the glass jar on the mantelpiece in my room. If this went on, I would have to buy a leather jacket and helmet and, like the youngsters at Eastney Youth Club, just pretend I had a motorbike.

~

Bathed, shaved, shampooed, Old Spiced, blow-dried and quiffed, I was coming down the stairs on my way to a Commercial Road rendezvous with my new mates from Eastney Youth Club when Mother popped her head out of the kitchen to ask where I was going. When I told her about picking up a new pair of jeans, I casually added that I was also thinking of picking up a small tattoo.

In those days, no girls and only silly sailors and hard nuts wore tattoos. Like a drape jacket or a cold stare, tattoos were a challenge. A good example were the members of the Earring gang. They were a fearful bunch who roamed the Landport area of the city and had a big reputation for violent behaviour. They had gypsy connections and were all short of stature but very long of drape jacket. As a hunting pack they struck fear in the hearts of pub landlords and dance hall customers. All sported earrings and tattoos and, each would wear a small swift or swallow, displayed on the left hand beneath the thumb. It was not exclusive to the Earring Gang, but a common symbol to declare you were a man not to be messed with.

As you will have noted, my mother had always been more than indulgent to my whims and wishes. But the idea of me branding myself for life was truly beyond the pale. She strode from the kitchen, blocked my exit, then led me into the sitting room, sat me down on the sofa and closed the door.

Over sixty years on, I can remember her expression and exact words.

If, she said in level tones, I came back with a tattoo, I would not be allowed in the house. Ever again.

Of course she would not have stuck to the excommunication order if I had turned up with my small tatt, but the threat was enough to make me change my mind. That was to be one of the rare occasions I made the right decision, but it was of course made only under duress.

~

A long, dirty and tiring day and I was glad it was Friday.

My dinner was on the table in the kitchen, and

beside it a copy of the Portsmouth Evening News. It was open at The Motor Vehicles for Sale or Wanted section, and I saw that one advertisement had been ringed in pencil. I looked closer and saw that it was for a 1953 Velocette MAC 350cc four-stroke. The asking price was £25.

'Is that the sort of thing you would want?'

Mother was standing behind me and laid her hand on my shoulder.

I nodded, and said more than a little bitterly: 'Absolutely, but it's a couple of month's wages. What chance have I got of saving that up?'

'Well,' the dear precious lady said, 'I know you find it hard to save, but I'm fed up watching you leave home before we're up and coming home so late and looking so tired. You fell asleep over your dinner yesterday.' She paused, then said: 'If you promise to wear a helmet and ride carefully, keep out of fights and not make any girls pregnant and never even think about having a tattoo, I'll lend you the money. Would you like that?'

I nodded dumbly and could have cried. In fact, I hugged her, went to my room and did.

Postscript and Trigger Warning

Thanks for joining me on my journey through my and my beloved city's life during the very different era of the 1950s. The next episode - *Pompey Lad II: The Rock 'n' Roll Years 1961 – 1965* is waiting for your kind attention. Just to let you know that it is a tad on the racy side. Where necessary, names have been changed to avoid embarrassment for others or a punch on the nose for me, but it is, as unlikely as it may seem, all true. There's a taster of Pompey Lad II at the end of this book, and I look forward to you joining me for what may or may not be the final chapter in my memoirs of times gone by.

The King of Rock 'n' Roll

With no warning, we lost Elvis on August the 16th, 1977. He was just 42.

As with the assassination of President Kennedy, millions still remember exactly where they were when the King left us. I was at the local radio station, Radio Victory, and went straight into the recording studio to scrap the planned edition of my programme *Pompey Rock* and replace it with an hour devoted to Elvis hits. On the day, I remember looking from the studio window and watching a small crowd gather in the car park to listen to the show and share their sadness.

As well as remembering the announcement of his passing, I, and I bet many millions of fans can remember where I was and what I felt when I first heard the King sing. And what it did to my head and heart and body. At just short of six feet and with an inimitable voice and almost impossibly handsome, he was the perfect rock idol. Unlike poor Cliff, he could also move like no other. He really was sex on legs, and unbelievably, a really nice bloke. We boys didn't resent his captivation of all those millions of female fans. We just wanted to be him... or as much like him as we could manage. Most of us couldn't manage the looks, the voice or the leg movements, so we had to try to match the hair. My first Elvis quiff appeared when I was 13, and I was to spend the next five years trying to perfect it.

With sales of a billion records and more than thirty movies to his credit (some quite watchable), Elvis Aaron Presley was an ever-present influence in and on the lives of my generation. We lived and loved with and to his music, and for us, he truly was The King of Rock 'n' roll.

Minding your Language

Portsmouth is a treasure trove for anyone wanting to sample a whole range of dialects, slang and other alternative uses and abuses of the Queen's English. We Pomponians talk so funny for a number of reasons. To start with, the city has been a premier Naval port for many centuries and the Royal Navy has a language of its own. Also, generations of naval ratings arriving in Portsmouth from all parts of the British Isles have left their regional linguistic mark. Then there is the picaresque linkage with London, and Portsmouth has long been a popular stop-off point for travelling folk. All these elements have combined to create an often impenetrable argot (even to some locals) which blends rhyming slang, Romany, naval patois and all manner of regional dialects. Here's a sample of Pompey street-talk, which is bound to attract some controversy and disagreement. This is because words used and precise definition and even pronunciation can vary in different parts of the city. In fact, I have known Pompey families who have their own private language.

NB: *Please note the usual disclaimer that I am only the messenger of how we spoke in the Sixties, and did not*

---

invent or necessarily use the more offensive ways of describing people or places. It was another time, and as they say, the past is like a foreign country where things are done and said differently.

Bok: From the Romany language and simply meaning 'luck', but used in Portsmouth in a negative form to mean the act of bringing bad luck or the person who brings it. My dad claimed my sailor uncle was a bok for Portsmouth FC as they always lost when he was in port and went to Fratton Park.

Brahma: There are various spellings but only one pronunciation for this word, which can be used as a noun or adjective. Broadly, it means something or someone of outstanding quality, as in 'What a brahma ruby' (*see below*) or 'She's a right little brahma.' Unlikely, I would have thought, but it may have some connection to the impressive bull of that name. One of the three major deities in the Hindu pantheon bears this name, which may also have some bearing on the matter.

Cushdy: Another Romany expression, broadly meaning 'good'. You might make a cushdy bargain, or say that someone has had a cushdy result. Sometimes the word is used on its own in reaction to hearing of someone's good fortune, as in 'Did you hear about Baggy? He's moved in with that brahma-lookin' nympho widow who owns a pub.' An appropriate response would be: 'Yeah? Cushdy...'

Dinlow: Fool, idiot. Often used in the short form of 'din', and can also be used as an adjective as in 'You dinny tosser.' I am told this is yet another Romany word with common currency in Portsmouth.

Iron: A gay man. One half of the rhyming slang 'Iron hoof' for 'poof'. Other and seemingly limitless non-pc allusions included shirt-lifter and turd burglar. Lesbians may be referred to as muff-divers or minge-munchers or even carpet biters. There is a well-loved if apocryphal tale that, in the 1970s, an anonymous wag took a small ad in the For Sale section of Portsmouth's daily newspaper. The clearly naive young lady who took the call duly typed it up and it appeared next day as follows: For Sale: One muff-diver's helmet. Only slightly used. The lovely thing was that her bosses could not reprimand the staff member who took the call for not knowing such an improper expression.

Lairy: This is a very common way of describing an irritating and sometimes aggressive general attitude, as in 'he's a lairy bastard.' Alleged to originate from mid -19th century cockney 'leery', and said to be common to south of England, particularly coastal areas.

Laitz: A state of absolute rage, as in 'he went absoloootly laitz, didn't 'e?'

NB: *Another London-esque linguistic custom in Portsmouth is to end statements with a question, as in 'I've gone down the road to see the mush, 'aven't I, and he's only done a runner, 'asn't 'e?' Origin unknown.*

Muller: To murder, but used mostly in a benevolent setting as in 'I could muller a pint'. Allegedly, the expression derives from the name of one Franz Muller, who committed the first murder on a British train when he killed and robbed Mr Thomas Briggs, a banker, on the Brighton Railway in 1864. Muller was hanged later the same year in one of the last public executions at Newgate prison in front of a mostly drunken crowd said to number 50,000. The murder resulted in the introduction of corridors to link railways carriages and the establishment of emergency communication cords. Again, the expression is said to be common to the South coast.

Mush: (pron. 'moosh'): An address to any male friend, stranger or enemy, to be used as in 'Alright, mush?' to a mate, or 'What you looking at, mush?' to someone you would quite like to hit. Again said to come from Romany, and is now somewhat dated and generally being replaced with greetings to friends and strangers by 'mate'. 'Mater' may be used with a particularly close friend. 'Matey' has more or less disappeared, but was for hundreds of years reserved for people who worked in the Naval Base, as in 'Dockyard matey.'

Oppo: A naval term for a close friend. According to the most likely source, it is short for 'opposite number' and referred to the man on board who did the same job as you during another watch. It paid to become friends for all sorts of reasons.

Pawnee: Rain. Corruption of Romany parni for 'water' and pani for 'rain'. Allegedly also from the old Gujarati word for water, picked up then corrupted by British troops in the early days of the Raj.

Ruby: Fairly modern and universally popular rhyming slang for 'curry'. Derived from Ruby Murray (1935-96), a husky-voiced Belfast-born songstress at the peak of her fame in the late 1950s.

Scran: Food. Credited generally to the RN via Liverpool or Newcastle, but also said to derive from Romany.

Shant: As with skimmish (see below), a noun or verb referring to ale or beer. Some Scots claim it as their own, others attribute it to the Royal Navy.

Shoist: Free, gratis. As in 'How much was your car?' 'Shoist, mater - I nicked it.'

Skate: Any Royal Naval rating. The term allegedly comes from the 18th century practice of nailing a fish of that name to the mainmast on long voyages for use by the crew in the absence of any obliging females on board (the genitals of the skatefish are said to be very similar to those of the female human).

Skimmish: Alcoholic drink, but usually confined to beer. Apparently peculiar to Portsmouth, but origin unknown.

Spare: Apart from the obvious, this word has two main uses. A 'bit of spare' is an available single female. To 'go spare' is to lose one's temper in an explosive manner.

Sprawntzy: Smart, well turned-out and confident-looking. Origin not known, but 'sprawny' is Polish for efficient or self-assured.

Squinny: Once again, a word which can be used as a noun or a verb or adjective. You can squinny or *be* a squinny. Basically it means whinge or whine about something in particular, or to generally be a moaner. According to academic sources it is a derivative of the word 'squint' and came into common use in the Middle Ages, but I am not convinced.

Wheee: According to decades of research (by me) this word/expression is absolutely unique to Portsmouth. As 'Well I never' might be employed in more refined circles, 'wheee' is brought in to play as a reaction to any piece of information or gossip from the mildly surprising to the truly shocking. Thus it would be used in the same way but with a different level of emphasis if someone said their bus was late that morning, or the next-door neighbour had formed a satanic circle and taken to keeping goats in the back garden for sacrificial and other purposes. I have asked people from all across the country, Britain and the world to try it out, but they can never replicate the depth, subtlety and variety of meaning conveyed by a true Pompeyite saying 'Wheee...'

Yonks: A long time. Like so many other examples, apparently imported into Pompey lingua franca by the RN. Some respected etymologists claim it comes from 'donkey's years'.

Acknowledgements

When I began my research, I planned to give credit to everyone who responded to my on-line queries and about their memories of Portsmouth in the 1950s and 60s. In practice, the list contained more than three hundred names before I even got close to the finishing line. All those kind enough to respond to my surveys and volunteer details will know who they are and my sincere thanks to you all. Photographs have been credited where possible, and a special mention is owed to George Langton, old school mate and local historian. Finally, there's the creator and devoted guardian of Memories of Bygone Portsmouth, JJ Marshalsay:

Memories of Bygone Portsmouth
https://www.facebook.com/groups/36600555020 1426/

Other sources include:

Portsmouth Past and Present:
https://www.facebook.com/groups/14298372039 69076/members/

History in Portsmouth - The Cooper Allen Music Archive
http://historyinportsmouth.co.uk/events/cooper-allen/1949.htm

A brief History of Southsea by Tim Lambert
http://www.localhistories.org/southsea.html

The Portsmouth History Centre
https://discovery.nationalarchives.gov.uk/details/a?_ref=42

The Popular Music Portsmouth Scene
http://michaelcooper.org.uk/C/pmsindex.htm

A Tale of One City
http://www.ataleofonecity.portsmouth.gov.uk/gallery/

According to one website, there are precisely ninety-seven novels and non-fiction works about or set in Portsmouth. Make that a round hundred, as the list does not include the first three of the Inspector Mowgley Murder Mystery series, written by no other than me.

The list can be found here:

https://www.mappit.net/bookmap/places/341/portsmouth-england-gb/

One of the books is 'Pompey', by Jonathan Meades, published by Vintage Books. It deals with the same era as this memoir, and has been acknowledged as a modern masterpiece. Potential customers should be advised it is not easy reading, and was described by critics as both brilliant and disgusting. A bit like the things people say about our city, then.

Other References

http://www.localhistories.org/southsea.html

Celebrities and famous people from the City of Portsmouth (welcometoportsmouth.co.uk) –

https://welcometoportsmouth.co.uk/famous-people-from-portsmouth-3.html

Portsmouth – Wikipedia
https://en.wikipedia.org/wiki/Portsmouth

And finally, everyone is entitled to their view, and here you can find some of the things the author does not like about Portsmouth. I would agree we could do without some of the listings, but we could certainly not do without the sea - and especially my dear old mate Fred Dinenage.

Why-portsmouth-sucks-a-list.html

Extracts from Pompey Lad II
The Rock'n'Roll Years

On Being a Biker:

Nowadays, Harley and Davidson. Honda Electra Glide, Motto Guzzi and other superbikes are almost common.

In our day, it was really something to own a powerful, quick bike with a legendary name. You'd see them at coffee shops and transport caffs in Portsmouth where bikers liked to gather and talk of compression ratios and re-bores and the like.

One of the most popular gathering places for those enamoured by big, big-name bikes was Bert's Cafe. Alongside a long, wide and mostly untroubled road on the outskirts of the city, Bert's specialised in fry-ups, bacon sandwiches and doorstep-sized slices of dripping toast. The mugs were man-sized and the tea strong, and Bert's was the in place for bikers to gather to show off their bikes, tell tall tales and indulge in regular 'burn-ups.' This was when you took on another bike in an urban road race.

A particular speciality at Bert's was the round-the-roundabout challenge. This involved the contestant sitting astride his bike with the engine running while someone put a specified record on the juke box. The challenge was for him to race towards the city, past the Smith's Crisps and Johnsons baby powder factory, round the roundabout there and then back to Bert's before the record ended. In those days, most pop songs lasted less than three minutes, so it was rare that the deadline was beaten.

I was half-jestingly challenged once, and to the

surprise of the regulars picked up the metaphorical gauntlet. This was not because I fancied risking my neck, but fancied a greasy biker's long-legged and big-breasted pillion passenger. Ever the dramatist, I chose Tell Laura I love Her as my record. The theme of doom-laden Ritchie Valens song was of a love-lorn teenager who dies in a car crash, and had been briefly barred by the BBC for fear it might encourage listeners to commit suicide.

With a soulful look at the curvaceous bikerette, I squared my shoulders, turned up the collar of my jacket and left. Although I thought about pretending to do the full journey, I decided to have a real go at beating the time challenge. Though limited to sixty-five mph top speed, my bike was no slouch at acceleration. Accordingly, I roared off and took what I thought were near-insane risks overtaking and cutting-up other road users. Back at Bert's, I dropped my bike on its side when I arrived and rushed in to hear the dying strains of Tell Laura I Love Her. The balloon of my elation was pricked when the referee told me I had taken so long he had put the record on twice…

On Coffee Bar Society:

Tommy Steele found fame at the 2i's coffee bar in Soho. My solo career started and finished on the same day at the Expresso Bongo in Arundel Street.

The classiest and oldest dedicated coffee house in Portsmouth was Verrecchia's in the Guildhall Square. People of all ages had long gathered there to drink in the incomparable bouquet of freshly roasted beans and delicious vanilla ice cream. There was also the posh Continental Café nearby and the Swiss Café in Edinburgh Road, but elsewhere it was generally caffs or tea rooms.

Then, in the early 60's, coffee bars became all the rage as meeting places for youngsters too cool to go to youth clubs and too young to go to pubs. All around the city, former groceries, haberdasheries and cycle repair shops were being refurbished, kitted out and given exotic names. Some had real Espresso machines for making frothy-topped milky coffee. Those on a tighter budget made up the latte of the day with energetic stirring and making gurgling sounds in the kitchen. Coffee was served in see-through cups and saucers made of the same glass as ovenproof dishes. They were supposed to be unbreakable but that did not always prove to be true, and were the source of many bad jokes involving Pyrex and Durex.

Café society would sit for hours eyeing up the talent across the rim or even through the cup, and I became almost addicted to the drink and the settings. I would do the rounds of the Expresso Bongo, Matador, Beachcombers, Delmonico's and Manhattan...and the even more exotically named Esperanto. They were the places in which to be, to see and be seen and sometimes entertained by local performers like Jon Isherwood and Pat Nelson.

To get in on the act and despite my lack of talent, I summoned up the courage and took my Hoffner Club guitar along to the Milano and laid it casually on the table. Unfortunately, or perhaps not, there was nowhere to plug the amplifier in and the place was filled with bikers playing rock anthems on the juke box.

They and the owners did not take kindly to my

request to turn it off, so I mimed a few hits like Kon-tiki and Apache while doing the Shadow walk and left the actual playing and performing for another day that I secretly knew would never dawn...

On Street Fighting:

Perhaps it was my disenchantment with my job or the lack of success with the band and putting my willy where I felt it belonged, but my life was becoming increasingly punctuated by acts of violence. Often initiated by me, but sometimes I was just the victim.

This was why one Monday morning I found myself sitting in a dentist's waiting room, feeling particularly sorry for myself. I'd been given a kicking, lost a chunk of a front tooth and been thrown through the window of an off-licence. To make things worse, I had to pay for the window, and even worse I was innocent of the reason I was thrown through it.

I'd expected just another evening when I tarted myself up, put on my Italian box jacket suit, and visited a youth club in Albert Road. I was still spending more time in youth clubs than pubs; not because I couldn't get in, but you had more chance of pulling a bird in a youth club than in most pubs. To summon up the nerve to smooth-talk a suitable victim, I would take a couple of pints on board before arriving. On this occasion, I had downed at least one too many rough ciders. I certainly felt no pain when I was set on by three youths who I was on nodding terms with. It started with a head butt and then a rain of punches and I went through the window of an off-licence.

Next door to the shop was a coffee bar run by a

tough middle-aged guy called Jim. He arrived, broke the one-sided fight up, staunched the flow of my blood with a tea-towel and asked what the scrap had been about. The regular girlfriend of the main protagonist was a pretty little blonde girl, and he said I had been seen chatting her up. When he had approached me in the street, I had attacked him and his mates and they had done no more than defend themselves.

I honestly could not remember talking to his girlfriend or setting about the trio, but looking for trouble after a few pints was to become a bit of a trademark for me in coming years.

This was getting silly. For the second time in a month, I had been attacked in the street by superior forces. On this occasion I'd been innocently standing by the milk machine in Milton Road after a game of darts in my local when a Triumph 500 screeched to a stop on the other side of the road. The rider and passenger dismounted, and I assumed they had stopped for a carton of strawberry-flavoured milk. In fact, they had stopped to give me a kicking. The rider had taken his helmet off and swung it at me before I had a chance to drop my drink and defend myself. Despite how they depict it in cartoons, it's not true you see stars when you get a heavy blow to the head, but I certainly saw some flashing lights. As I went down, the pillion passenger kicked me in the stomach, and through the pain I noted how almost balletically it was done. As I sensibly stayed down and lay there with arms over my head, the rider used his steel toe-capped knee-length biker boots to give me another one to the guts. Before they left, he picked up my carton of milk and poured what was left in it over my new, four-button pin-stripe Italian Jacket.

As I watched them through a rapidly closing eye, I saw how differently the pillion passenger walked from the rider. The buttocks in the tight blue jeans were swaying with each step and I realised I'd been kicked while down by a female.

The next day I took my new jacket into the cleaners, and when I told the boys about the incident I didn't mention that one of my assailants was of the opposite sex. When I wondered why they had attacked me, the general view was that I had committed some offence against them, but little Mac pointed out that even at a distance and doing nothing, I looked really lairy...

On early DJ-ing:

Though hoping the new group would be my passport to fame and fortune, I was now even more concerned about my lack of musical ability. It would be a bitter blow if, like the Beatles' drummer, I was dumped when the Rockin' Hot Rods made their big breakthrough.

Then it occurred to me that though I couldn't sing or play an instrument, I could ride to success on the back of someone else's music. I was a big fan of Radio Luxembourg disc jockeys Emperor Rosco, Stuart Henry and Johnny Walker, and would practise my patter by dipping the volume on my transistor radio and talking over their introductions to the hits of the moment.

Though crap with any form of music-making, I seemed, as Granny Kelly would say, to have the gift of the gab, and I reckoned that if the band went tits-up or I was chucked out, I might be able to make a name for myself as a disc jockey. I'd already worked out what that name should be, and predictably it was King George. As it transpired, my on-the-road performances were not a success, and I had no idea that in a decade or so I would be hosting rock 'n' roll programmes on and helping run Portsmouth's first local radio station. Unlike managing bands, I seemed to do well shaping Radio Victory, if you don't count it being the first ever local commercial radio station to lose its license. But, also again, that's another story.

Then, and without any kit except my tranny radio, I was learning the trade at local youth clubs. I'd arrive with an armful of my favourite records and take over the gramophone. If there was a microphone, I'd do my DJ bit…which even then I thought was sometimes bum-clenchingly awful in its banality. Kenny Everett was an inventive genius; I, like Smashy and Nicey, was just a copycat, churning out the predictable cliches in a phoney mid-Atlantic shout. The members at the clubs I imposed my act on did not always take kindly to my tastes, and one evening it got physical.

I was strutting my stuff at St Margaret's Youth Club in Highland Road, playing Hard Hearted Hannah by the Temperance Seven when a big, tough-looking young man came up to the stage and beckoned me over. I bent down and asked him if he had a request, and he said words to the effect of: 'Yeah, stop playing that fucking crap and put something good on'.

One thing led to another, and it being a church hall

and deserving of respect, I invited him outside to continue the discussion. Following him towards the door and looking at how really big he was, it occurred to me that I was out of my depth. For the first time and to my shame, I took the coward's way and got the first blow in by hitting him from behind. Within seconds I was grabbed, thrown across the foyer and slammed up against a wall. I found myself face-to-face with a young black man, who smiled engagingly as he drew his be-ringed fist back. As if this was not bad enough, I looked over his shoulder and my bowels moved. Looking on and also smiling was the younger brother of the famed and feared Pompey Ted, Hughie Finnegan. I had obviously just thumped one of his gang.

I shut my eyes and awaited retribution, but the punch never came. Later and when we became close friends, Patrick Finnegan told me that the reason he and Don Price were smiling was because I looked so terrified, and it seemed a shame to punch somebody so obviously shitting himself...or nearly shitting himself. At the time, as he reminded me, I had gabbled out my apologies and said how I was a fan of his brother, then let out a massive fart of fear.

As I have said before, it was often strange how we met and made friends in those days...

On Portsmouth Pub Life:

A new set of mates, and a new place to meet them.

In what was to become a pattern, I had moved on from one group of friends to another, and my life began to revolve around pubs, drinking, chasing crumpet and fighting. Since my escape from retribution at St Margaret's church hall, I'd started to hang around with Pat Finnegan, Don Price and their mates Ray Wheatcroft, Jackie Grant and Mickey Wicks. Inevitably we were to become known as The Finnegan Gang.

Along with a number of similarly-minded young people, our local was the White House in Milton. We would travel around other pubs in the area, but Wilkie's was our HQ.

Before the War, there were more than a thousand corner pubs, taverns, ale-house and gin palaces in Portsmouth. With no telly and sometimes no heat at home, a pub was somewhere you went to nurse a drink and keep warm, socialise, celebrate special occasions, or just get drunk. Thanks to the Luftwaffe, re-development and the shrinking of the Royal Navy, hundreds of Pompey pubs had disappeared. But every area of Portsmouth still had more than its fair share, and because of Fratton Park and the Royal Marine barracks, Milton and Eastney had more than most.

The White House was an unremarkable-looking hostelry, flat-fronted and plain, with none of the over-the-top features of the Brickwood 'folly' pubs. The front elevation was unsurprisingly painted to suit its name. A decade ago it transmogrified into a small terrace of unremarkable town houses, and doesn't look as if it was ever a busy boozer.

What happened within its walls still stays in my memory, and when passing, I sometimes wonder that there is not even the tiniest echo of its past life left. It seems wrong that all that is dead and forgotten, and I think how fitting it would be if the residents might occasionally hear a ghostly bell clanging for last orders, or smell the fug of stale cigarette smoke and beer and hear the echoes of laughter and singing and a fragment of 'At the Hop' on the juke box as they open their front doors…

~

This was to be the decade of great social change, but in the early Sixties, pubs were still much of a muchness. Lino on the floor of the Public Bar and carpet in the Lounge or Saloon. The off-licence or Bottle and Jug was where you picked up a packet of crisps, a bottled beer or even a couple of pints in a bath jug. In the Public there might be a shove ha'penny board and bar billiard table to go with the darts board, but juke boxes or any sort of musical background were rare in the more traditional corner locals. All ale was 'real', and lager beer had yet to take over the counter-tops.

Apart from the odd pub offering scrumpy cider, the choice on tap was limited to Mild or Bitter. Bottled beers would include Light and Brown Ale or the stronger barley wine, and ladies could enjoy a half-pint glass of shandy or, lately, a Babycham.

Spirits were generally reserved for Christmas or special occasions, as were port and lemons and something yellow and sticky called an Egg Flip.

Catering was mostly limited to crisps, jars of pickled onions and eggs and the odd meat pie or a Scotch Egg. The lack of gastro-pub catering in Portsmouth would be noticeable for another twenty years. We took our first Pompey pub in 1983, and when I asked the outgoing landlord about catering arrangements, he said they did a few sausage rolls and pies, but them little round things with cheese on top were getting popular. He was I later realised, referring to pizzas...

On Driving, Drinking and Drugging:

Another now-shocking aspect of life in the foreign country that was Britain in the Sixties was how socially acceptable it was to drink and drive. And how acceptable it was to drive a death-trap. The yearly MOT had arrived in 1960, but only tested lighting, steering and braking.

The idea of setting a legal limit to how much drivers could drink and testing to see if they were fit to be behind the wheel only came in with the arrival of the breathalyser in 1967.

Nowadays it is socially unacceptable and accepted as just plain wrong to drink or drug drive; in the early years of the decade, the idea of being behind the wheel while tipsy or even blind drunk was quite literally a joke. When a pub regular was so plastered he could hardly stand and someone asked if he would be able to get home safely, the usual response was: 'He'll be fine - he's got the car with him.'

The road casualty and death rate at the time reflected the shockingly casual approach to drink driving. It's a sobering thought that in 1968, nearly 8,000 people were killed on Britain's roads. Nowadays and in spite of the huge increase in traffic, the figure is around 1500. My new group of mates were even more culpable, as we drove under the influence of drugs as well as drink, often both at the same time. Miraculously, lamp posts, trees and hedges were the most common victims of the insanity, and I survived a dozen potentially fatal collisions when I or another member of the gang was driving. My guardian angel must have been on duty, but not for many others...

While we band members chose French Blues or Purple Hearts to get us in the mood for a performance, the chemical stimulant of choice at the White House was found in an unlikely setting.

Chemists' shops in the area must have thought that there was a long running epidemic of head colds and blocked noses. The reason for the sales boom was the discovery that the cardboard strip in a popular brand of decongestant tube was soaked in amphetamine. Nowadays used to treat narcolepsy, ADHD and obesity, Benzedrine was then used to help clear blocked nasal passages. For those in the know, a tube of Nostriline was a lot cheaper than buying 'benny' in tablet form, and would keep the user awake and alert and raring to go for the weekend. The way of ingesting noz was a matter of choice.

Some people tore a piece from the impregnated card and swallowed it down with a draught of beer. Others liked to put it in a stick of chewing gum. However we chose to take it, the intention was the same. To get and stay up for the weekend without losing a minute to sleep.

Little, of course, is really new. Nowadays young people like to take Ecstasy or put white powder up their noses. We used the secret ingredient inside a tube that normal people stuck up their noses to help them breathe more easily...

Pompey Lad II 1961 – 1965 The Rock 'n' Roll Years, is available on-line or to order at any reputable book retailer.

Printed in Great Britain
by Amazon